The House by the Sea

The House by the Sea

A Portrait of the Holocaust in Greece

Rebecca Camhi Fromer

Mercury House
San Francisco

Published in the United States of America by Mercury House, San Francisco,
California, a nonprofit publishing company devoted to the free exchange
of ideas and guided by a dedication to literary values.

United States Constitution, First Amendment: Congress shall make no law
respecting an establishment of religion, or prohibiting the free exercise
thereof; or abridging the freedom of speech, or of the press; or the right
of the people peaceably to assemble, and to petition the
Government for a redress of grievances.

Mercury House and colophon are registered trademarks
of Mercury House, Incorporated.

Design and typesetting by Thomas Christensen and Kirsten Janene-Nelson.

Printed on recycled, acid-free paper and manufactured by Hignell Printing Limited in Canada.

This book has been made possible in part by generous support from
Merry Belden and from the Maurice Amado Foundation.

Library of Congress Cataloguing-in-Publication Data:
Aelion, Elia
The house by the sea : a portrait of the Holocaust in Greece /
Rebecca Camhi Fromer.—1st ed.
p.   cm.
Includes bibliographic references (p.)
ISBN 1-56279-105-2 (paper : alk. paper)
1. Aelion, Elia. 2. Jews—Greece—Thessalonikē—Biography. 3. Holocaust, Jewish (1939–1945)—
Greece—Thessalonikē—Personal narratives. 4. Thessalonikē (Greece)—Biography.
5. Thessalonikē (Greece)—Ethnic relations. I. Fromer, Rebecca. II. Title.
DS135.G73A45   1998
949.5'65—dc21
[B]   98-4382
CIP

5 4 3 2 1
FIRST EDITION

Cada patada tiene su sombra.
Each step has its shadow.

SEPHARDIC PROVERB

I am indebted to Michal Friedlander, Curator of Judaica at the Magnes Museum in Berkeley, for bringing to my attention a communication she received from Andrew Apostolou in London, at present deep in research for his doctoral dissertation on "Bystanders and the Holocaust in Greece" at Oxford. Through her efforts I was able to establish direct contact with Mr. Apostolou, who lost no time in providing a copy of the declassified document to be found in Appendix F. The unearthing of this document required painstaking diligence, and yet Mr. Apostolou offered it to me without hesitation and in the best tradition of enlightened scholarship. This document is of utmost importance, and my appreciation is boundless.

Contents

Illustrations

Elia Aelion. *Salonika, 1945.*

Preface

Elia Aelion is a modest man whose easygoing manner does not lead one to suspect that he has a story of consequence to tell. Thanks to the power of memory and its cherished images, however, and thanks to diligence on the path, we have been able to reconstruct the elements of a way of life that is no more, but once was rich indeed.

This is not a mythology or a work of fiction. If the reader hears poetry, it is because Elia has a poetic soul; if the reader hears romance or sees mischief, it is because these, too, are Elia's qualities. This is a serious work that is grounded in its purpose to convey the aroma of the past, the tenor of the struggle to survive, and the nature of the loss in Greece due to the Holocaust.

In invoking the first person, I have been able to both reach into another's life, becoming part of it, and sharpen the critical faculties necessary for such a work. These faculties consisted mainly of a heightened sense of awareness in detecting continuity or incongruity in the telling of the tale. As such, they formed the basis of our dialogue and inquiries.

As in other works, I have not used a tape recorder. In any case, we were not conducting interviews. We spoke as the storytellers of old, without impediments, and in earnest to inform.

Each chapter begins with a Sephardic proverb, and the reader will find the original Ladino within the text. My translations convey the essential rather than the literal meaning of each, but the internal rhyme scheme could not be conveyed in English without considerable damage to the thought.

The House by the Sea

Introduction

To explain the convoluted geopolitical situation of the people and region in which the events we are about to explore occurred goes well beyond the scope of our intention and deserves full development elsewhere. Suffice it to say that we are speaking of a complex arena of inquiry, the product of which is our subject.

Despite numerous incursions, conquests, and reconquests over the ages, the sweep of time has allowed for a certain constancy to prevail along with the changes brought about by war. One of these constants seems to have been that the city of Salonika, in present-day Greece, remained a part of the Ottoman Empire from the mid-fifteenth to the early twentieth century. Its inhabitants were citizens of Turkey and were treated well, although non-Muslims paid taxes and were subject to other regulations and minor restrictions, which were often disregarded. In contrast to the tense relations that existed between the Turks and the Greeks or Armenians, relations between Jews and Turks were relatively relaxed.

During the Balkan Wars of 1912–1913, Salonika was ceded to Greece, and by 1922 to 1923, as a result of the Treaty of Lausanne, a significant exchange of population took place: the Turks left, and the Greeks returned after a lapse of more than four hundred fifty years. Where once the Sephardim—Jews who could trace their heritage to Spain and Portugal, dating back to 1492 or 1497—had been the overwhelming majority, they now found themselves inundated by the influx of more than one hundred thousand Greeks. The nation had changed hands, but the mores of the people were of the past. Jews, who had lived in the area for centuries and who had developed excellent ties with the Turks, most of whom were Muslims, spoke many languages, among them Ladino, or Judeo-Spanish, French, Italian, and Turkish. They spoke no Greek, but, as they acquired the necessary skill to do so, they also acquired a distinctive accent that immediately identified them as Jews. This "signature" proved to be catastrophic during the Holocaust, and the following pages will make this point abundantly clear.

Salonika was a main center of Sephardic life and culture, not a mere outpost of Jewish survival. The Sephardim were active in every manner of endeavor, and a command of their language, Ladino, was essential. They had their range of poor to rich, as in all societies, and they had their councils; they had their communal institutions, and they discharged their duties. They were responsible, hard-working, philosophical, and flamboyant.

When the Greeks came en masse, they found the Jews occupied in seamanship, exports and imports, wineries, the weaving of silks, woolens, and other textiles, law, medicine, scholarship, etc. They were in the professions, but they were also grocers and tailors, bookkeepers, salesmen, and common laborers. Everywhere the Greeks looked, the Jew was evident as an integral part of the fiber of life—and many resented it. They outnumbered the Jews, but they had not established the network or structures that in fact do not crop up overnight—and their envy or hostility, under wraps for perhaps a decade, played a heavy role in the Holocaust. It simmered and seethed, possibly unconsciously at first, but when the Germans overran Salonika and the oppression began, Jews there rarely encountered the extent or quality of sanctuary that the Greeks of Athens or smaller towns and villages so willingly gave. In those areas, it has been argued, the situation differed because Jews were not so dominant. As we shall see, however, the good-hearted sow the seeds of humanity wherever they are, and a compassionate few were to be found among the Greeks of Salonika, even as they were to be found among the Italians who were allied to the Germans—and some of these will find their way into our pages.

The Jews of Salonika went into hiding if they could, often fleeing to Athens, the hills, or remote villages—sometimes referred to as Free Greece—far from the heavy presence of the Germans in the north.[1] Many young men and women joined the partisans or served in the Underground, but many more could not abandon their families; these remained behind, did what they could under the circumstances, and were swept away by disease, starvation, slave labor, random acts of sadism or violence, and other atrocities. By August 18, 1943, the nineteenth and last transport to leave Salonika emptied the city of its Jews. It had taken a little less than five months to decimate a great culture.[2]

The Jews of Athens, along with those who went there seeking asylum, also went into hiding; their presence was an open secret, and everyone conspired to keep them both safe and comfortable. Upon the capitulation of the Italians on September 18, 1943, however, this situation changed radically. The Germans came in force, the ruses began, and the roundups or terror of the *razzas*[3] followed. On April 11, 1944, the first transport left for Auschwitz, and on June 30, 1944, the remainder of the Jews of Athens went to Auschwitz along with the Jews of Korfu.[4]

In 1940, prior to the German invasion of Greece from Bulgaria the following year, the Italians attacked it from the Albanian border. Within the existing army of defense at that time were some four thousand Jews from Salonika, and Elia was among them. From 1939 to 1941, he served

Elia as a recruit in basic training (standing, fourth from left).
Salonika, 1939.

as a quartermaster; his rank was that of sergeant first class, and, as an inductee in 1939, he underwent the usual basic training. This training took place in Salonika, and directly from there he was sent to Fano.

On October 20, 1940, the Italians, who had lost the war they waged with Albania, were ordered to invade Greece. The Italian campaign was on, but the Italians fared no better in Greece than they had in Albania; they retreated or surrendered, and at times entire divisions capitulated to one or two Greek companies. Perhaps weary of war, or in fear of maltreatment or being shot in reprisal, they came forward with upraised arms, pleading: *"Perché? Perché?"* as if to say: "Why shoot us? We don't want to fight you!" As a result of incidents such as these, Mussolini's well-known boast that he was "sitting on eight million bayonets" was subjected to crude ridicule.

On April 6, 1941, when the Germans invaded Greece,[5] Elia was in an area between Bulgaria and Yugoslavia, where the Greek army, routed by the Germans, had fled in disarray. He was not in the immediate war zone.

Germany's invasion of Greece was a boost to her Italian ally and furthered the larger aim of conquest. The attack was sudden, swift, and vigorous, and the Greek army at Fano began to plan its retreat toward Klisura, high up in the mountains above Kastoria and south of Florina.[6] In anticipation of the withdrawal, Elia, who was in charge of a company of two hundred fifty men, was to bring provisions to a designated rendezvous point. Nearly twenty-five mules were loaded with supplies from one of seven warehouses, and the men set off. Their officers had arranged for them to sleep on the cemetery grounds of a church along the route, and the next day they arrived at their positions.

At Klisura the opposing armies engaged in battle, and the Germans defeated the Greeks. Animals strayed and food was lost, officers fled and entire units retreated. The men headed for Lake Ostrovo, where they hoped to reorganize, but their efforts proved to be futile. After the stunning defeat at Klisura, it was assumed that Greek traitors had divulged strategic information that led the Germans directly to the new position deep within a mountainous region, across tiny bridges and on narrow roads, a location impossible to find without direction. The Greek army was now in a state of collapse.

Elia and several men from his unit escaped on foot and walked for days from the region of Lake Ostrovo to Naupflion, a distance of some three hundred miles. There they hid for two or three days, during which time they encountered very few of their comrades. Both the Greeks and the English stationed at Naupflion strove to repatriate the army, hoping to direct it to the Middle East, but when the Germans bombed the liberty boats in which the men were to be transported, the plan had to be abandoned. At this point, Elia removed his officer's stripes. He and his men had been ordered to engage the enemy, but the capacity to do so did not exist. The Greeks and the English capitulated or dispersed, and the Germans now began to shower Greece with flyers disseminated from the air. In essence, the sheets proclaimed: "Go to your homes. Everything is okay." In fact, it was not. The Greek army had fallen apart at Naupflion, and the Germans, who at that juncture had launched their blistering attack from Yugoslavia,[7] rolled their triumphant tanks through the heart of Salonika within three days.[8]

Elia, his friend Salvatore Benveniste, and a comrade wandered aimlessly through the streets of Naupflion. They did not know what to do, and they were very frightened. Each was still in uniform and consequently in grave danger of being detected. A stranger offered to help them: "We'll do something about this," he declared, and he took them to his home. The men, however, remained fearful. They did not know this man or whether he could be trusted, but no other options presented themselves.

The three had been embraced by a sympathetic family. They were fed, given a place to sleep, and provided with civilian clothes. Thus outfitted and encouraged, the following morning they set out for Athens. The trains were still operating and they went directly from Naupflion to Athens, which would have to do. Salonika, where they wanted to be, was out of the question. The Germans were on the march, and the roads belonged to them.

The three jumped aboard an open cattle train, entirely packed with soldiers like themselves, and rode for hours. In all that time they could do no better than to stand on one foot. When the train at last came to a stop, Salvatore and Elia went one way and their comrade went another.

Elia and Salvatore headed for the Atlas Hotel, which was a refuge of sorts frequented by Jewish families. They were now so weary, unkempt, and full of lice that the manager turned them down when they asked for a room. If they hoped to stay, they were told, they would have to bathe, discard what they wore, and get into clean clothes.

The two friends went shopping and to the public baths, dressed satisfactorily, and were accepted by the manager on their return. They could now concentrate on how to get back home. With all means of communication between Athens and Salonika cut off, the near impossibility of getting gasoline even if by an unlikely stroke of good luck a vehicle should offer itself to them, and no money, they were prepared to work hard to achieve their goal.

One day Elia heard a curious tale. A bus driver from Salonika, whose bus and sole means of support had been commandeered by the Germans, succeeded in tracing it to Athens and was determined to reclaim it. This he somehow achieved by one means or another, but he had no money, the bus had no gas, and he desperately wanted to return. Toward that end, it was reported that he was prepared to take anyone to Salonika who could provide a five-gallon container of gasoline. This was sufficient for Elia—and for days afterward, both he and Salvatore strove diligently to secure the necessary "currency."

The story of the bus driver had been an improbable one on several counts, but the bus driver, the bus, and the fact that the two friends were homeward bound were real enough. On the road, the charmed life of the vehicle yielded yet another tale to the saga of the bus, for once again the Germans tried to confiscate it. This time, however, due to the extraordinary tenacity of its owner, everyone was allowed to proceed unharmed.

At last Elia arrived. His destination was the home of his parents, and his concern was to avoid shocking them. He therefore sought a friend who would go to the house and tell his parents that Elia was well, and that he had seen him in Athens—but the friend did not do so. What he conveyed was that Elia was not only in Salonika, but also waiting at the corner, out of view, behind a little wall where he could see what was happening. Within moments, Elia was deluged. His mother and father, sister and brother ran to him, and in a rush of joy, the first words he heard were those of his mother, who said: "I knew you would come! I made you some new pajamas!" It was now May, 1941, and a few weeks into the German occupation of Salonika. Within days Elia would be busy at work in an earnest effort to salvage what he could of the family business, and in short order, after returning from a trip to Volos on just such an assignment, he would find the house empty and his mother in tears. The Germans had stripped the house, taking everything, including the light fixtures. Only the beds remained.

Not long after this incident, Elia would return to Athens, delegated with the responsibility of effecting as smooth a transition as possible for those in the family who hoped to escape the oppressive conditions that prevailed in Salonika under the sometimes understandable but more often incomprehensible, haphazard, seemingly capricious behavior of the Germans. The pacing and intent of German priorities were not understood, but in Athens—under an eminently more humane administration in the Italian zone—they hoped to survive in the exercise of care.

What was going on in Salonika?

On April 12, 1941, three days after German columns overran the city, the German army requisitioned a certain number of Jewish homes and apartments, took over the Jewish hospital, and closed the offices of the Jewish Community Council; on April 15, eight of the Jewish Community Council members were arrested and community records were confiscated; on April 17, other Jewish leaders were rounded up and arrested; on April 20, the Germans instituted an anti-Semitic newspaper and published its first editorial blaming the Jews for ruining Germany in the aftermath of the First World War; on April 29, they ordered the Jews to turn in their radios; on May 1, they requisitioned all shops owned by Jews and arrested their owners; on May 12, they openly encouraged acts of oppression by Greek anti-Semites. On May 17, they arrested Rabbi Koretz—whose later counsel would prove to be ruinous to the Jews[9]—and on May 22, they both appointed a weak individual to head the community and en-

"Sunday Morning 'Sport.' It is of advantage to head the group as guard is in the rear. Labor had no use since there were no roads. Primary target was to weaken the prisoners' resistance."[11]

dorsed a statement by the Greek prime minister, proclaiming that Jews and non-Jews would be treated alike—an evident falsehood. By June 29, German scholars from Berlin arrived to inspect the rare books and manuscripts on hand in Jewish academies, synagogues, and private homes. As a result of their efforts, tens of thousands of precious volumes were expropriated and sent to Germany—but where these texts are today, no one knows. On that same day the Gestapo further requisitioned Jewish homes and apartments, and a Jew was executed for beating a German soldier.[10]

"Irritants" such as these continued to occur until the onset of much more serious repressions. On July 11, 1942, in an incident that took place

Black Sabbath. Three men in foreground: right, Samuel Jacob Rouben; middle, Leon Jacob Rouben, his brother; and left, unidentified. Leon was heavyset and could not keep up with the pace of the "sport." Sam, who was younger than his brother, tried to help him. For this, the Germans beat him mercilessly, leaving him bloodied and bruised. His wife, Mary, tended Sam's wounds for an entire week. Leon never spoke of the event. *Liberty Square, Salonika. July 11, 1942.*

in Liberty Square involving the roundup of some nine thousand Jewish males of Greek citizenship, the first open display of German sadism made its appearance. The decree issued by the Germans for that day required all male Jews of Greek descent to gather in the square, presumably to register for work assignments. From eight in the morning until two in the afternoon, they were made to do "sports" under the broiling sun of an oppressively humid day. Many collapsed; they were neither allowed to wear caps or sunglasses, drink water, or use the facilities, nor were they to be aided by anyone. As each man fell, the Germans poured buckets of water on, bruised, kicked, stomped, maimed, or killed the uncomprehending victim. SS soldiers attended by huge, ferocious dogs moved among the crowd, amusing themselves by ordering Jews to disrobe, dance, or exercise in groups. Some were made to roll around the square, like barrels, in a naked state. From time to time, Germans released the dogs to tear at the naked men on the ground. Above the square and on the rooftops of the buildings bordering it, German officers, in full view of those below, stood at their posts with machine guns in hand or in charge of small caliber cannon, there to effectively quell any rebellion.

By February 6, 1943, the racial laws were promulgated; by March 20, the first transport of twenty-eight hundred Jews left the railroad station for "work in the East," and by March 25, two ghettos were instituted so that the Jews could be "autonomous." This was, of course, no more than a ruse to isolate those they feigned to protect and soon transported to their deaths.[12]

The Italians warned the Jews to flee, issued passports and false identities, or otherwise sought safe houses for them; in addition, they affected a certain ineptitude in implementing the directives of the Germans. In so doing they invited the animus of their allies, who turned upon them after they capitulated.

For the Jews of Greece, as for Jews and others elsewhere in Europe, the final calamities were ferocious. The last moments of revelation blotted out the sun, and removed man far from the comforts of illusion.

Rebecca Camhi Fromer
Berkeley, California

Notes

1. For the most part the Italians were in the south and the Germans in the north, but each had a detachment or so at either end.

2. Because the ratio of Sephardic deaths due to the Holocaust falls into the highest category of any group, the following bears consideration:

a) Not understanding the German language, the Sephardim could not follow orders or comprehend anything said to them, but the camps were places where instantaneous responses or hesitations meant life or death, or the rewards and punishments that led to one or the other.

b) The Sephardim were taunted by the Jews of Eastern Europe, who generally withheld from them any feeling of solidarity. Unable to believe it was possible for a Jew not to know Yiddish or not to be of their culture, Eastern European Jews repudiated the Sephardim. Since the formation of coalitions who "organized" for survival were a factor in survival, and since one needed to orient oneself as quickly as possible, this lack impacted heavily against them.

c) The Sephardim came from a warm climate and could not cope with the severe winters of Eastern Europe.

d) Most of the Sephardim went directly to Auschwitz and their deaths. Since the crematoria were functioning at optimum efficiency during this period, few were "given the opportunity" to be slave laborers.

e) The brutal rigors and sadism connected with the Death March sufficed to demolish all but a small number who had managed to survive up to this point, and these few could not comprehend how or why they had lived.

3. The *razzas* were random acts of violence in which the element of surprise was crucial. The Germans swooped upon Jews as they walked in the streets, herded them onto waiting trucks at gunpoint, and transported them to slave labor or concentration camps.

4. Among them were four hundred young men, who were killed immediately because they refused to do the work of the *Sonderkommando*. This "special command" unit at Birkenau-Auschwitz was a slave labor detail whose prisoners worked in the gas chambers and crematoria, clearing the cadavers from crammed gas chambers and cremating them after removing hair and gold teeth. They were made to smelt the gold for shipment to Germany and to dispose of the ashes by dumping them in the Vistula River under heavy guard. The *Sonderkommando* were slated for systematic execution at regular intervals until the last months of the war, during which time the Germans accelerated the genocide of the Jews.

5. Yugoslavia was invaded by the Germans on the same day. Refer to "The Holocaust of Yugoslavian Jews" in *Sephardim and the Holocaust*, (Gaon and Serels, eds.), p. 64. Eleven days later, on April 17, 1941, the Yugoslavians capitulated.

6. Refer to the map on p. 156.

7. Bulgaria served as the springboard for the attacks on both Greece and Yugoslavia. For its cooperation it received as "trophies of war" a slice of Greek Thrace, a part of Yugoslavian Macedonia, and the city of Pirot in Serbia (see Gaon and Serels, 36). The Bulgarians did not fight; they collaborated.

8. The Germans easily overcame Athens as well, but they then delivered it to the Italians for occupation. Refer to Susan Zuccotti, *The Italians and the Holocaust* (New York: Basic Books, 1987), 97–98.

9. Rabbi Koretz allayed the fears and outcries of the outraged community. In urging compliance to avoid further disaster, he in effect worked against resistance or escape.

10. The following anecdotes share an ironic component, each of which is instructive: Some time during this period Sula Broudo Benveniste positioned herself directly across the street from Gestapo headquarters. She reasoned this was the safest place to be and, with an assumed identity card, she felt reasonably comfortable sitting in a chair in front of the house, where she developed the daily routine of knitting. Her parents, too, were in hiding, each quartered separately.

All went rather well until one of the SS officers fell in love with Sula and proposed to her. Sensing the inherent danger in such a situation, Sula fled and went underground.

At about the same time, Jack Kakis lived next door to where the Gestapo had set up their offices—and for him this was too close. He chose to move, with the aid of a friend. This proved to be profoundly amusing to two SS officers, who smirked as they held on to their dogs' leashes. The officers, believing their dogs had been trained to detect "the smell of a Jew," looked on approvingly and in glee. The dogs had not barked or attacked, and thus the SS men supposed "the Greeks" were stealing Jewish property.

Kakis joined the partisans, while other members of his family joined the Underground. Among the latter, was his sister Carmen.

11. From *The Book of Alfred Kantor*. The ironic use of the term *sport*, as well as its inhumane applications, followed the civilian victims into the concentration camps, as evidenced in Kantor's sketch of recalled events and numerous other sources.

12. While the Greek Orthodox priesthood exhorted the Greeks not to humiliate the Jews—particularly after the promulgation of the racial laws—Queen Frederika, the queen of Greece and a Nazi sympathizer, openly paraded in the uniform of the Hitler Youth.

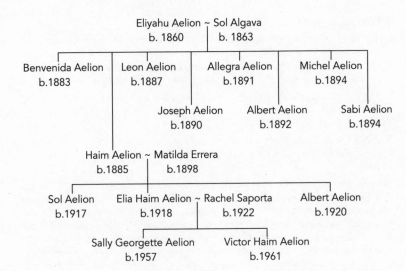

Eliyahu Aelion ~ Sol Algava
b. 1860   b. 1863

Benvenida Aelion   Leon Aelion   Allegra Aelion   Michel Aelion
b.1883   b.1887   b.1891   b.1894

Joseph Aelion   Albert Aelion   Sabi Aelion
b.1890   b.1892   b.1894

Haim Aelion ~ Matilda Errera
b.1885   b.1898

Sol Aelion   Elia Haim Aelion ~ Rachel Saporta   Albert Aelion
b.1917   b.1918   b.1922   b.1920

Sally Georgette Aelion   Victor Haim Aelion
b.1957   b.1961

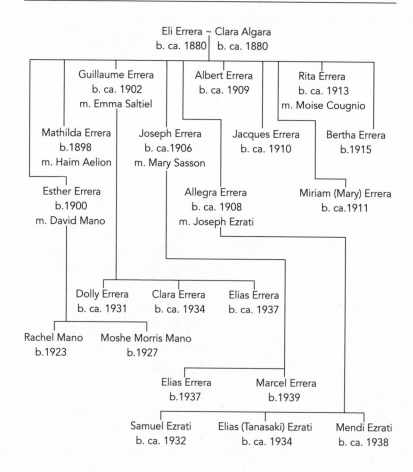

I

Il sueño no tiene dueño.

A dream has no master.

I was born in a house that sat at the edge of the sea and stood on four cement pillars. It was a house that was filled with people and laughter, the cries of mischievous children, and the whispers of adults, who shielded us from the mysteries of life or grown-up cares. The house was a haven to us despite the fact that on the upper story lived a man by the name of Venezia[1] who acted strangely, reveled in frightening us children, and who once dumbfounded everyone by sawing off a rung of an external ladder meant to serve as a fire escape. Perhaps he was a bit mad and perhaps he was merely eccentric; I do not know. (He flashes through my mind like a rush of rain in springtime, colorful as a rainbow.) The house had a spirit of its own, and we imbued it with our essence. We loved it passionately, and its steady ways cultivated in me the great but mistaken notion that I lived in an ordered, safe, and relatively sane world.

The house was as inseparable from the sea[2] as we were from it, and both aroused in

1. There were many Venezias in Salonika. This Venezia does not refer to any of those depicted in my book *The Holocaust Odyssey of Daniel Bennahmias, Sonderkommando*.

2. This is to be taken literally; it is not poetic license. Because of the tides, the lower floor was deep in water most of the time, and was always vacant. Stormy weather only exacerbated the problem.

me a sense of well-being—a feeling for something that may be called eternal constancy, and those sentiments that give one a clue as to what constitutes the good life. All that seems worthwhile, warm and loving, simple, innocent, and natural were generated there and implanted into my awakening and fertile consciousness. Its nonexistence is unthinkable, and to this day the reality of the house and its many ghosts survive in a memory untarnished by the gripping turbulence of the ensuing years. My mother and her sisters and brothers—Esther, Guillaume, Joseph, Allegra, Albert, Jacques, Mary, Rita, and Bertha, whom I always called Berta—were raised within those walls; I have been fondled, chastised, and cared for by all of them, and it was there that I first knew the intoxication of the salt air and felt the tantalizing mist, there that I sensed the tide rip the shore and naughtily threw my shoes into the beckoning water, there that my child's heart palpitated to the percussive dance of the slats on our blinds when the strong winds rattled them into puppetlike tremors clattering away in a chattering frenzy.

To this day I can picture my grandfather, whom I called *nonu*, fishing from the veranda that ran the length of the house, a large bucket filled with water resting at his feet. I can see how he cast his line and reeled in his catch—like a true fisherman—and how, at the end of the day, he overturned the bucket. Out poured the unwary fish who had taken his bait. Day

after day he stood so, and day after day the
fish were redeemed and sent tumbling back
into their elements. Quite content at his ac-
complishment, *nonu* smiled: "How often
can we eat fish?" Awake or dreaming, I picture the terrace on the second floor that also
ran the length of the house and faced the sea.
I see the tables laden by *nona* (my grandmother), my mother (Mathilda), and one or
another of her many sisters, and all of us
meeting there—ravenously hungry—to eat
our meals, the sun above, the comfort of a
soothing, cool breeze about us, and a vista

Nonu with one of the
Counio children.

of breathtaking, awe-inspiring beauty that revealed
the arc of the sea stretching out into infinity. To the
left, delineating the horizon, were the large ships sail-
ing on to ports unknown, and to the right, the sweep
of the city of Salonika.

The house had settled over the years, as if in obei-
sance to the sea, and we could feel her sway in unison
with the oncoming night, the pulsating stars, and the
tugging of the luminous moon. I ran and played and
teased within her arms and within view of her sagging
frame, and I was a source of grief at times—no, I was
not altogether a "good" boy—but all the many people
who dwelled within the great heart of this house were
too close to harbor feelings of lingering injury. There
were differences between us, as in all families, and

there were angry episodes—occasionally with me at the root cause of the problem—but the barriers of pride and displeasure at wrongdoing did not last. The healing and reuniting of family, and that kind of solidarity, superseded all other considerations and could not be breached other than temporarily.

Mine was an idealized life, a life of "reasonable" indulgence at the hands of doting parents to whom I had a special—but not sacred—status. This may have been due to the fact that I was a sickly child and had not been expected to live, so that when I foiled death it was seen as a sign of some sort, an indication of a charmed life, or a miracle. Neither my elder sister nor my younger brother was treated as preferentially as I was, but then there seemed little need for that; they were healthy, and I was not. Still, I was not immune to disciplinary correction, mild as it was. My father took no hand in such matters, but my mother "came after me" *con la pantufla,* with her slipper—a soft affair. How unconscious of their efforts my parents and relatives were as to their role in my eventual recovery! When I collapsed in the street and they carried me to safety or safeguarded me in countless ways, it was considered a natural response and of no special consequence. When my mother took me from one city to another, where we stayed for up to two weeks each in an attempt to gradually build up my resistance to disease, that too was felt to be in the order of things. I was fed cod liver oil, raw eggs, and bananas, and I was exposed to every manner of "cure," but never did they dream that my charmed life consisted in the miracle of the love they lavished on me so unstintingly.

Because the house fully captured my imagination and because my identity with it is so complete, I am sure to convey a wrong impression—for I did not live there from infancy onward. Among my earliest memories I still remember the sensation of being nestled into a basket and carried off, and to this day I am convinced this recall marks the point of our departure from my grandparents' home to our own—some five minutes or so away.

The house we moved to was in the suburbs, on Mizrahi Street—a principal, tree-lined thoroughfare near the Baron de Hirsch Hospital.[3] Midway between my home and my grandparents' home and on the same street was *La Scola Alcheh,* the private Jewish school I attended along with my brother and sister. Here we studied both Jewish and general subjects, with an emphasis on business education. Distances were close, and I went to the house by the sea as often as I could. It drew me like a magnet.

Because so much about the *scola* was unique, I would like to say a word about it. First of all, boys and girls were on the same grounds, although they did not attend class

3. A huge compound, which the Greeks took over in a "forced sale" after the war. Taking advantage of the Jews' predicament and the weakened state or essential destruction of the community, they "purchased" the hospital for a mere pittance—basically stealing it.

in the same building. Second, the curriculum for girls and boys was the same in all essentials, and both were bound by the same rules in matters of deportment.

I do not recall what it was that I was guilty of at this particular time, but I do remember that, whatever it was, it fell on a day when the entire school was scheduled to go on a picnic. The principal, Mr. Alcheh, was very disappointed in me, and would not allow me to go along with the others. My punishment was therefore confinement, and I went to "jail" for the duration of the outing. This jail consisted of a room within which I was locked, and which actually had bars on the door. One of my parents had to pick me up, but it was always my mother who came for me—and this time was no exception. As was often the case, my mother's grief at my mischief had been an adventure for me, a way of getting attention—and one that I treasure to this very day for its very innocence.

Halfway between my home and the *scola* was the *Matanoth Laevonim* (Gifts to the Children), which happened to be on Mizrahi Street too. The first floor of this building was devoted to eating facilities, and the second floor to a facility that could be rented out for weddings and special occasions. At some distance from here was an orphan asylum with a capacity of about one hundred beds. These children, or the orphans living with an uncle or aunt or other relatives, or the children of the poor, came to the *Matanoth Laevonim* by tram or bus or on foot. They came in

Albert Aelion, in the front row and wearing a white shirt, about to leave by train on a class outing. Four instructors as well as the school's founder and principal, Isaac Alcheh (second from right, standing), accompany the boys on what is most probably a senior high school event. *Salonika, 1937.*

streams and from all directions to eat lunch; this was an everyday affair, and we sometimes joined them. What is of great interest here is that it was the custom in the community for an individual to pay for all of the children's lunches on the *yarzeit,* or commemoration day of one's father's death. Everyone so affected tried to perform this *mitzvah,* or act of charity, but it was not always possible to do so.

A short distance from the *scola* was the *kehillah* (synagogue); a few yards from that was an intimate study house for the pious and the scholarly, and a few feet from that there were the tram tracks. I remember very well a revered old gentleman called *Tzadik, il ciego* (Pious, the Blind), who came to study each day and had to be assisted so that no mishap befell him—particularly at the spot where he had to cross the tracks to get to the study house. One day, his heart broken over his infirmity, he cried out, imploring the Almighty to relieve his plight—and on that day alone, he was able to cross the tracks, go home unaided, and arrive unscathed. This impressed me, and I have often wondered about it.

My father was the president of the synagogue, and my mother attended services from time to time. We were not especially religious, but we were identified with and very respectful of tradition. Twice a year—during *Succot* and *Pesach*—the men in the family took the children to visit one another's homes, while the women remained behind to host those who came. It was customary to serve ice-cold water, orange glacé, homemade preserves or *charope,* a sugar candy, and baked eggs—colored brown, Sephardic style. A silver tray of delights was passed around, and confections were served in crystal ware and eaten with silver teaspoons. Since numerous children were in each family cluster, these visits abounded with human energy. On *Erev Yom Kippur* we met at the house by the sea and, after breaking our fast the next day, we met again. *Nona* served *pastel de calavasa* (squash pie). The day of Yom Kippur itself we turned on no lights and handled no money. We met again at *Purim* in order to read the *Megillah* at the *Kehilah.* If by chance the

Megillah fell to the floor, the individual from whose hands it dropped had to fast for twenty-four hours. Once, when this happened to me, my parents consulted my grandparents, both of whom upheld tradition, sure in the knowledge that I would come to no harm. Thus, though I was delicate, I was not exempted from the obligatory as a matter of course.

We were all from Salonika and most of us stayed there until the advent of the Holocaust—but some had gone to Palestine before the war, while others had gone to France. After the war only one had survived on my mother's side of the family, and very few were left on my father's side. Of those who did not survive, I particularly remember the fate of my aunt Allegra's three small children, one of whom had contracted typhus during the epidemic of 1941. Allegra, who was a young widow, nursed him but came down with it herself, and subsequently died. My maternal grandmother, Allegra's mother, took one child under her wing, my uncle Joe took another, and my parents took the youngest. The family had rallied around the children and had drawn them in close, but to no avail; the three could not be shielded from the Holocaust. Two died in the gas chambers of Auschwitz, and the third was burned alive in one of the pits at Birkenau-Auschwitz.

My mother and father were first cousins. My father was fifteen years my mother's senior and had ten siblings—one sibling more than my mother. One day my paternal grandmother spoke to my maternal grandmother, her sister, and said: *"You know, last night I had a dream . . ."* The content of that dream saw one child married to the other—and so it came to be, for the dream was seen as an omen. Fortunately my parents loved each other and had a happy marriage, but I found it very strange that my father never called my mother by her name or expressed endearments like *honey, sweetheart,* or *darling.* (As to how it was between them in private, I cannot say.)

My mother was a beautiful and intelligent woman. She wrote in and spoke French, and was fluent in Ladino. She loved to read and go to the movies, and was very strong, very competent, and I remember her as the disciplinarian in the family, a woman secure in her domain and in the knowledge of her worth.

My father worked for the firm of Aelion, Rousso, and Botton, a company that "gambled" by buying ten acres of grapes in winter in the hope of having a good harvest in summer. The company made raki, uzo, cognac, and other liqueurs and ran a small cannery that preserved anchovies in large wooden vats. It was a modest business by American standards, and many of the items they produced were sold from a little retail shop attached to the plant. Since my father also served as the president of the corporation, he devoted a great deal of time to the job. When he needed to nap, he went to his office. He sat in a chair, looped an arm

Elia's mother, Mathilda Errera Aelion, and his sister,
Sol, in *Purim* costumes. *Salonika, c. 1921.*

around a chair to either side of him, and stretched his legs on a fourth chair in front of him. Seated thus, his head rolled back, his body slumped, and he napped. If asked: "Why do you lie here like this?" he simply replied: "Because I like to." As we grew older, my brother helped my father at the factory and I free-lanced, taking advantage of my special status as my brother fulfilled or exceeded expectations.

Perhaps my father was overprotective of my mother, or perhaps it was just convenient or the custom of the day, but my mother did not do the shopping. My father bought fresh fruit and vegetables daily, and had Chaimiko,[4] who worked at the store, deliver them to the house. Five days out of the week, Chaimiko took the tram—a ride of some fifteen minutes each way—laden with wholesome things to eat. On his return to work, he carried the lunch my mother had prepared for my father in what was called the *sefer tasin* (the book pot),[5] three pots that hooked onto a metal frame.

4. *Chaimiko* (Chāimikō) is diminutive, and an affectionate form of address. It stems from the Hebrew word *chaim*, signifying life. Like altogether too many others, Chaimiko was killed in the Holocaust.

5. *Sefer* (Hebrew), signifying "book"; *tasin* (Turkish), signifying "pot." Perhaps derived from the meals scholars and pious men brought with them to the synagogue on the Sabbath, when they remained there all day long.

When I was about twelve and at my grandparents' house, I remember taking a rather insistent position with regard to my cousin Rachel's panties. "What color are they?" I teased over and over again, but Rachel—intuiting an ulterior and somewhat prurient motive on my part—stubbornly denied my budding curiosity the least satisfaction. Quite the contrary. She shot out of the room and dashed through the house with me yelping at her heels, and within moments I was catapulted into disgrace.

The house I loved could be bitter cold at night and so, in addition to our wood-burning stove, which was inadequate to the task, we commonly resorted to a huge brass brazier for the warmth we craved. Now, this brazier, which we lit out of doors so as to keep the rooms free of fumes, took on the semblance of a rite when brought in, held on high, and positioned onto a stand outfitted with foot rests for those who could sit nearby and brave the most intense heat, but on this day, everything went awry. My cousin Rachel was on a collision course with my aunt Berta, who—at the very moment of impact—was carrying the brazier with its cache of burning, bright red coals.

Berta remained steady as Rachel crashed into her, gashing her own chin so that it later required four stitches. Fortunately, however, not a single coal toppled. Although no one and nothing was burned, the glare of everyone's anger singed me. *"Por la luz del dio, te vo cortar la cavesa."* "By the light of God, I'll cut off your head," my mother screamed—and, irrational as it may seem, for long weeks afterward there were hard feelings between my aunt Esther—Rachel's mother—and my mother.

Although we did not know it then, these were to be among the last sparks of our existence. In time and strictly by chance, Esther and her husband, David, as well as Rachel and her brother Maurice made their way to Palestine.

My grandparents worked hard, as one well may imagine with so large a family, and made every sacrifice to educate all their children. They were unable to do so, however. My grandfather was a simple grocer who imported grains and sold olive oil. Unstable economics and political upheaval beset him like any man, and yet he strove to send three sons abroad to study in their chosen fields. Although two aspiring pharmacists and one physician went to French and Swiss universities, the drain proved to be too much. The business that could not support such outlays failed, and the two who worked to be pharmacists could not complete their studies. Thus Guillaume alone succeeded, and returned home a physician.

My aunts and uncles always saw to the needs of their parents. "Here, Ma, take this," they would say as they handed over various sums—but, strangely, my grandmother had no use for money. She rolled the bills, tied a band around them, and put them in a trunk or drawer, or under a mattress. Maybe she had grown unaccustomed to anything but the basics and counted her riches in other ways, and maybe she meant to leave the money for her children and grand-

Elia's grandparents at Joseph and Mary's
wedding at the *Matanoth Laevonim*.
Salonika, August 6, 1936.

children. Long after the liberation, only the trunk my
grandmother had entrusted to a friend came into my
possession. I could not bear to open it, and it remained as it had been presented to me for many years.

II

A la guerra, la ley quede cayada.

In war, law is silent.

As I grew up, I was more concerned with my sister Sol[1] than with my brother Albert. A mere year separated Sol and me; we were close; we were alike in temperament, and I provided an acceptable means for her to be with boys—something a "good" girl from a "good" family did not do indiscriminately. Each of us looked out for the other; Albert, the youngest, took care of me, and I watched over my sister. Thus, while we loved one another deeply and without reservation, I regret that I did not have the opportunity to do anything special for Albert.

Although Sol and I were inseparable, she infringed on my independence, and there were times when I felt that in responding to her needs I had sacrificed a part of my own youth. She clung to me and cried: *"Ke va fazer yo si ti vas?"*[2] if I wanted to be with one friend or another, but if it was Baruch it was particularly unsettling. She loved him. An exquisite tension filled the air as each was drawn to the other, and as a consequence Baruch and I did far less together than we might have. Later on, how-

1. *Sol* (sōl), from the Spanish word signifying sun.

2. The *f* in *fazer* is indicative of a possible sojourn of Jews in Portugal. It is a constant presence in one strain of Judeo-Spanish, or Ladino. Thus we may see or hear *fijo* in place of *hijo*, etc. The phrase itself means: "What will I do if you go?"

Albert, with Sol to his left and a friend to his right, at a local park.
Salonika, c. 1937.

ever, I understood and had a better, more tolerant view of their yearning for one another.

When the Germans overran Greece and took full control of Salonika, Baruch and Sol faced inevitable separation. The transports for "work in the East" had been initiated[3]— and Baruch, who had been too young for conscription in the Greek army, now had to contend with the new regime and its "requirements." Since married couples "had the privilege" of taking the transport together, Baruch and Sol became husband and wife in name only and with the approval of both sets of parents. After the ceremony each returned to the parental home, and Sol's trousseau remained intact. They left together when Baruch's name appeared on the transport list, their union unconsummated, and were never seen or heard from again.[4]

Before these events and in an ironic twist of fate, I, who had been in Athens, had asked a friend of mine, an Italian officer, to go to Salonika in order to bring Sol to me. Before Italy's capitulation in 1943 we all knew that Athens—under the jurisdiction of the Italians—was much safer than Salonika, which was under the Germans (the situation changed radically afterward), and yet my father refused to let Sol go. He felt that she ran the risk of rape, and in her stead he entrusted

3. Unsuspecting the fate that awaited them, many of the Sephardim made their own *devantales* (aprons) in the belief that they were truly going to work.

4. Many such marriages took place during this period, and it was commonplace to say: *"No mi quiero morir sin gustar lo bueno de la cama."* (I don't want to die without first savoring the pleasures of the bed.) In some cases the will to live, to survive the camps, drew its inspiration from this desire, but of course the element of chance weighed heavily against such fulfillment.

the officer with a box containing precious items and some of my mother's jewels. These I received at his hands. When I wished to compensate him, he rebuked me: "What's the matter with you? I am your friend!" Such was his character. (What happened to him after Italy's surrender is unknown to me.) I had had the good fortune to meet a decent man, and as true a friend as anyone could hope for. At night he brought food to me from the canteen, and I leave it to you to imagine what this can mean in wartime when food is scarce and starvation rampant.

It seems incredible to me that I had the luxury of any adolescence at all in view of what was soon to befall us. What is more, I have trouble absorbing the fact that my memory serves as one of the few spiritual "proofs" of the once vibrant reality of friends and family. I had a friend Marcel, for example, who was in love with Elsa—a girl with a glorious mane that she often wore in a pony tail. She was very beautiful in many respects—and *I* liked her too—but because of Marcel, I never did anything about it. Marcel's habit was to plead: "Give me a kiss, Elsa. Won't you give me a kiss?" It was his way to call for her at her home and beseech her beneath her window, and hers to peer out of the window in response. Before long, Marcel's plaint would fill the air: "Elsa, give me a kiss! Give me just *one* kiss!" Each time he did this and to no one's surprise, Elsa pouted and uttered a petulant

"No," and then clamped her folded arms down onto the sill in unmistaken emphasis. One day Marcel, Elsa, a girlfriend, and I were seated on a bench in the park when Marcel began the usual refrain. Utterly dismayed by Marcel's ineffectual ritual, and perhaps a little in my own interest too, I grabbed hold of Elsa's pony tail, pulled her toward me, plunked her on my knee, and kissed her. "*See*, Marcel," I cried triumphantly. "You *don't* ask!" To my horror, both were killed by the Germans. They never had a chance.

Still another Marcel—this one my friend Marcel Nadjari, who was two years older than I and lived next door to my grandparents' house—was to have a terrible fate meted out to him. Because he was young and strong, and because Mengele selected him along with other young, strong men to be a slave laborer in the *Sonderkommando* at Birkenau-Auschwitz, he was made to participate in the Germans' process of annihilating more than a million Jews.5 Once upon a time we called him *"Marcel, il loco,"*6 because he was so funny—a true comic and the life of the party—and I will never forget how he did the tango, or characterized the affectations of that dance. All of us roared then, but in Birkenau he cheered the prisoners and made one or two of the Germans laugh at his antics—and this was extraordinary.

5. See Glossary and note #4 p.14.

6. Marcel got into everything and seemed to make decisions without thinking about the consequences, but this was deceptive. "How nice to have a boat," he would say. "Let's do it!" First he would get a rowboat, and next he would get a sailboat, in actualization of the dream. The phrase *"Marcel, il loco"* (Crazy Marcel) was used affectionately; he was loved by all.

Albert Aelion.
Salonika, 1938.

My brother, Albert, and his girlfriend and her entire family—save for one brother—were killed by the Germans. When I met this brother after the war, my heart was utterly empty. He was desolate, and so was I. Wherever we went, we were confronted by loss.

III

Il lobo troca il pelo, y las manos no.

The wolf sheds its hair, and not its hands.

Dr. Guillaume Errera.

My uncle Guillaume, the doctor in the family, was a guardian angel to me; he treated me when I was an infant and a child, and he watched over me as a young man. "Do you need money?" "No." "You *need* money." He underscored the words quietly, and unpretentiously pressed money into my hands or stuffed it into a pocket. He knew; he always knew, and he was always generous. "Do you need a suit?" "No." "*Come on,* you *need* a suit," he persuaded.

Guillaume had saved my life from I know not what disease, but he was more than a family doctor. He was the physician to the French branch of the Rothschilds, who gave him a series of medical tomes as a gift, and it was not uncommon for patients or physicians to consult with him. I can recall the dramatic case of a woman who had been referred to him when she was six and a half months into a difficult pregnancy. The local doctors had recommended that the baby be taken from her so that she might live—but when my uncle was called in, he contradicted their assessment and the family then consulted Viennese physicians. Their response to them was: "Do what

Guillaume says." At term, he delivered the baby. Both
mother and infant were alive and well.

My uncle knew medicine, and for the most part he
knew people too. One day, my grandmother found my
grandfather seated on the edge of the brass bed; he
was not well, and could not move. When Guillaume
came in response to her call, he looked at his father.
Later on, he spoke to his mother and said, "Papa is
going to die in three hours." And so it was. He could
be outspoken and protective at the same time. This
was his quality. When I took an interest in the heavy
medical books sent by the Rothschilds, he inter-
cepted me in the library. "Don't read that," he said. "I
don't want you to concentrate on the symptoms of
disease." He had warded me from the effect of the inference of disease, and I have wondered since then
whether or not he had done the same for himself too.
Is it possible that he "looked the other way" when dis-
sension and joylessness promised to destroy him?

Guillaume had three children and was unhappily
married to Emma, who came from a wealthy family.
She was more than distant, she was cold—and no-
body in the family liked her. Although she kept seven
persons on staff as either governesses or servants,
Emma was miserly and put little food on her table,
which baffled everyone. The family never visited,
she was never welcome, and—despite all unpleas-
antries—divorce was out of the question. Guillaume

alone had all doors open to him and I alone visited him at his office as a sort of liaison, bringing along with me news, the illusion of normalcy, and perhaps an antitoxin to the "disease" that bred within the cold walls of the cold house in which he lived. In time, and to no one's surprise in this instance, Guillaume developed a relationship with a woman whose sickly husband, a patient, soon died.

Guillaume, holding Clara, with his wife, Emma, resting her hand on Dolly's shoulder. *Salonika.*

At a certain juncture in the oppression of the Greek Jews at the hands of the Germans, Guillaume stayed in Salonika and went into hiding with Emma and the children. He paid a certain Mme. Boyer handsomely to bring food and essentials to them and, in addition, entrusted the greatest part of his wealth—which was considerable—to her care. Yet one day, during a period of great unrest and much looting in the streets, Mme. Boyer's greed got the better of her. "Oh, what a beautiful wool blanket that is," she remarked pointedly to my uncle in passing—and Guillaume understood her language very well. "Here, take it," he said. "You have done so much for us." Sadly, in his gift lay the undoing of an entire family. When the Germans accosted her in the street only moments later, she betrayed Guillaume and his

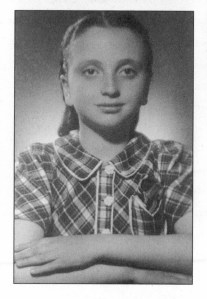

Clockwise from left: Dolly Errera, Guillaume's eldest child; Elia Errera, the youngest; and Clara Errera, the middle child. Opposite: Dolly and Clara in *Purim* costumes. *Salonika, c. 1936.*

family without hesitation. Witnesses later reported that when asked where the blanket had come from, she had tossed her head over her shoulder by way of indication and said, "Over there, from Dr. Errera." As a result, Guillaume, Emma, and the three children were rounded up at once. Their next address was Auschwitz, but not before Guillaume was severely beaten and no longer recognizable.

Emma and the children were killed in the gas chambers of Auschwitz, and Guillaume, who barely survived the indignities and servitude of the camp, was nearly forty when he died of typhus almost immediately after the war. A short while later, his mistress invited me to lunch. Nothing eventful occurred until I noted the presence of a little boy—a boy so like my uncle that when I fastened my eyes on him it took my breath away. To this she said, "The child is the housekeeper's." She refuted what I saw in plain view, offering in its stead an improbable tale. I therefore understood that she had wanted me to know something of Guillaume had survived the ruins, but that she did not want to be explicit. It was the Sephardic way—the way of indirection. She wanted no involvement and the matter was to remain closed. I saw Mme. Boyer too, for I expected an accounting of my uncle's estate from her, but she looked at me blankly. I was not there; I did not exist for her, so how could she possibly respond?

IV

La ida esta en la mano,
la venida no se quando.

My departure is in the palm of
my hand; my return is not.

My mother's brother Joseph was younger than Guillaume—and like Guillaume, who was something of a genius as an obstetrician, he not only excelled in business but also elevated it to an art. However hard he worked, something special entered—and whatever that special something was, it weaned effort from drudgery.

Initially Joe started out as a bookkeeper,[1] but later he entered into a partnership with a man by the name of Sarfati. Together they went into the sale of woolen yardage, with Sarfati functioning from Athens and Joe working out of Salonika. Clearly, while Joe liked to "make a deal," he loved to "play the game" even more—and every "maneuver" in creating a market was seen in chesslike terms, with the excitement of an enthusiast engaged in an utterly absorbing theoretical adventure. Only later did it become a matter of true master strokes, outwitting the enemy, and actual survival. This was especially so upon the dissolution of the partnership with Sarfati, at a time when I was directly involved in the drama of helping to salvage an amazing enterprise from the invasive Germans.

1. He worked for Daniel Bennahmias's maternal uncle, an Abravanel.

Left: Joseph Errera and Mary Sasson, with Dolly (seated) and Clara
(standing), before the ark at the *Matanoth Laevonim*. Top: Gathering
for Joseph and Mary 's wedding, in front of the *Matanoth Laevonim*.
Bottom: Elia's grandmother being helped by his
aunt Bertha (in white, with outstretched arm).
Salonika, August 6, 1936.

Before he married Mary Sasson, Joseph, who loved the arts, attended the theater and dined out. Afterward, his direction turned to his wife and her family, with whom they lived. Between us we used to say: "A Sasson did not become an Errera, but an Errera became a Sasson," in homage to the affection that existed between the two branches of the family. In due time there was his own growing family to consider—two sons, Eli and Marcel, and one of Allegra's three orphaned children, Tanasaki Ezrati. Thoughts of the theater and other arts receded, and war loomed large.

Joseph, like Guillaume, was the sort to whom family meant everything, and his heart was as open as his purse. One day after having seen that a certain young man who worked for him at the store might be the perfect match for his sister, Rita, a girl of uncomplicated mind, he approached him directly and said, "Moise, if you marry my sister I will set you up in business. I'll get you a store right across the street, and it will be yours." Now this fellow was a Counio, and no fool. After thinking it over and consulting with his parents, he countered that while setting him up in business was a satisfactory starting point, it was in no way sufficient. It would take time to build any business, and he had no staying power; he therefore required the Erreras to agree to what was called *la mesa Franca* (the French table), a common enough practice that found its way into many a dowry agreement. In short, the bride's family agreed to house and fully support the couple for an indefinite period. My grandparents, only too happy to help, raised no objections—and after the wedding, Rita returned with Moise to live with her parents at the house by the sea.

Little by little, Joseph built up a prestigious firm. He had an exclusive contract with Papageorgiou of Volos, Greece, the larger of two mills that produced woolen textiles—and he conducted a brisk, reciprocal trade with countless individuals to whom he loaned money so that they too could enter into the woolen yardage business. His terms were simple: the wool was to be purchased from him, and the loan was to be paid in five years.

Joseph's system worked well. It created friends and goodwill, as well as a name known to the extent that "when Errera bought wool," the price of wool rose on the commodities market. This last development was a mixed blessing, for when prices shot up, not even Joseph could afford to buy at the going rate. Detecting the potentially ruinous pattern early in the game, my uncle engaged me to buy wool, reasoning that an unknown entrepreneur making miscellaneous purchases would not make an impact on the market. I was instructed as to what to do, and was given enormous sums with which to pay for anything I bought. In this manner and for the time being, we averted disaster.

2. Only three days after invading Greece, the victorious Germans entered Salonika in motorized columns. The very next day all newspapers were closed down, and a fiercely anti-Semitic newspaper was installed "in their place" (*nea Evropa*).

3. On April 12, the Germans requisitioned homes and hospitals. On April 29, the Jews were informed through the newspaper to turn in their radios; on May 1 certain stores were requisitioned, with additional stores meeting the same fate on May 5.

On April 9, 1941, the Germans occupied Salonika, and from that time on our lives were not the same.[2] The Germans entrenched themselves and lost no time in taking what was not theirs.[3] Before long, they "discovered" Joseph's business; they came into the shop, took what they wanted, and gave every indication they would return. It was certain that if this practice continued without hindrance, the stock would be depleted—and Joseph now took the first of a series of steps to safeguard the woolens. He was determined to extricate the family from possible harm and avert financial ruin.

The first immediate step was admittedly primitive, laborious, and Sisyphean. The shop was housed in a five- or six-story building, and since that was all Joseph had to work with, he used it as a temporary expedient. Each morning everything but a few representational bolts was taken onto the roof, and each evening everything was brought down again and stored for the night. By day, the Germans could come to their own conclusions. They had not as yet taken inventory, and my uncle needed time.

Joseph made arrangements with the Amarillo Trucking Company[4] and had everything shipped to Athens. There were several points of delivery, and every one of them was to a non-Jew whom Joseph had befriended and helped to set up in business. Each one did what he could according to his means, with one individual able to safeguard as many as forty crates filled with material. Not one asked for recompense. My role in Joseph's plan was twofold. I was to leave Salonika for Athens, and at each point of delivery I was to create an inconspicuous, walled-in hiding place with access for mothproofing purposes and periodic maintenance. During this undertaking, I was also to find a safe house for everyone so that they too could come to Athens.[5] When I arrived, I had Joseph's list in hand. I knew where to go, and I knew what to do.

I did my job. I went from place to place and created walled areas behind which woolens could be safeguarded; I aired and mothproofed the fabric; I conducted trade, buying and selling and negotiating for goods other than those stored away; and I looked for a suitable place for Joseph. All transactions were in gold, and my money belt bulged with coins. In contrast to my experience in Salonika, I felt safe as a Jew and could move about freely. I wrote to my parents, and I was in telephone communication with them. Either they or I placed a call by prear-

4. A Jewish company, which deployed several trucks for the transportation of the goods. Note: *Amarillo* may appear as *Amariglio* in some accounts.

5. Joseph actually located the first safe house on his own. He had chosen to stay in the village of Loutraki, outside Athens—a place of relative obscurity. The husband in the household, however, made passes at Mary, who was very beautiful, and Joseph felt impelled to leave. He sent a note to Elia asking him to look for another place. The reference speaks of this juncture in the dynamic. Taken altogether, Joseph, Mary, and the children were in Loutraki for a period of between two to four months.

rangement at the central telephone company—a process that took a day or so. As Jews, we were no longer entitled to telephones of our own.[6]

The last time I spoke to my father was both harrowing and unforgettable. "They are at our door," he cried. "Keep our name alive!" By then, at least for him, the artifice of "work in the East" had been unmasked;[7] I had heard the presentiment of death in his words, and I was very upset. My parents, Sol, and one of Allegra's orphans remained in Salonika.

The hectic phone calls from Salonika to Athens and back again, the exchange of letters, carefully worded, and the courier waiting to help bring everyone down to

6. On February 6, 1943, a *Shabbat,* the SS promulgated the Nuremberg laws. All Jews from the age of five and older were to wear a yellow patch on inner and outer clothing, and Jewish businesses were to display a yellow Star of David. Jews were prohibited from changing their residences; they were to no longer use the trolleys, and they were to turn in their telephones. (The Jewish Community Council and doctors were not deprived of telephone access.) Radios were now finally confiscated, since the directive of April 29, 1941, had been widely disregarded. The overall purpose was aimed at accelerating the process of isolation, disconnecting the Jew from normal channels of communication. By March, 1943, the consistent stance promoted by Rabbi Koretz to comply with all German directives had kept in check the impulse to resist and led to a continued worsening of the situation. On March 17, the community gathered in the synagogue, demanding an accounting of him. The congregants were so infuriated by Rabbi Koretz's responses—which they construed to be lies—that, were it not for the intervention of the Jewish police, Koretz would have been lynched (Gaon and Serels, 82). By March 25 all the Jews of Salonika had to be in one of two designated ghettoes. These steps, taken nearly two years after the occupation, plus the fact that the ghettoes were to be policed by Jews as well as the encouragement to comply by Rabbi Koretz, led to a false sense of security.

Athens and relative safety—in short, all of our desper-
ate efforts to extricate ourselves from the Germans—
had come to no avail. We had had a plan, and it had
gone awry.

My grandmother and another of Allegra's orphans,
Berta, Albert, and Rita and Moise were at the house by
the sea. Not everyone could afford to go to Athens—
the payoffs were prohibitive—and not everyone was
capable of going into hiding. Despite the furious pace
of my efforts, it was not easy to convert cloth into gold,
and this is precisely what my family needed. The
drachma was worthless in the cities but not in the
countryside, and these were the days when I often
heard my Uncle Joe plead: "Sell goods! I need gold!"[8]

7. By this time, the entire stock in the Aelion, Rousso, and Botton winery had been
stolen by the Germans. Elia's father, Haim Aelion, had been made to load a large
truckful of anatol (the essence of the liqueurs), which was never to be seen again.
Treasured wines and liqueurs, aging in and covered with sand on the cool basement floor, were also taken. His father had never dreamed such persons existed,
and the mentality behind a confiscation of this sort was incomprehensible to him.
To be without assets closed the family's options; in effect, it placed escape within
the framework of the miraculous.

8. The plan was for Joseph, Mary, and the children to escape to Athens first;
Guillaume, Emma, and their children were to follow. The grandmother did not want
to leave Salonika, and the others could not leave because they did not have the
means to do so.
    When Joseph arrived with his family, Elia transferred the gold to him and he, in
turn, paid the courier. At no time did Elia meet the go-between. The same courier
responsible for the details of Joseph's escape was to have been used for Guillaume
and his family, who were ready at the time Mme. Boyer's betrayal foiled their plans.

V

Mil pensieros no pagan una devda.

A thousand worries don't pay a single debt.

At the time I arrived in Athens in 1941, I went to see my father's brother Leon, who had come down from Salonika on business and was staying at the Hotel Atlas. I had not found a place to stay as yet and I had no idea how long he would be here either, but I did not want to miss him. I reasoned that he would return to his wife and daughter as soon as possible, for he was very devoted to them.

On my way to the Atlas my thoughts turned to his daughter, Sol, who was a tomboy, and her brother, David, who was both elegant and eloquent and a hedonist and wastrel. The worst that could be said of Sol, who was much younger, was that she enjoyed breaking the neighboring windows with a pebble-and-string pendulum while perched on the limb of a tree. David, however, shamed the family. He caroused, maintained two mistresses in separate households,[1] dealt in the black market as a means of survival, engaged in dubious escapades—and became the gigolo of an older woman as debts consumed him, mistresses abandoned him, and the fortune he had amassed plummeted and finally vanished.

1. Both mistresses were actresses. One of them, Nana Skiada, was among the most famous actresses of her day, and we may infer that David was very wealthy indeed during this period.

I met my uncle at the hotel and stayed with him for a few days. During that time we took long walks together, and he confided in me. David's dissolute behavior disturbed him greatly, and he cried like the desperate father that he was. Grieving all the while, he struggled with conflicting emotions—so that one moment he was angry at David, and the next he wished for his regeneration. *If* only he came to his senses! *If* only he were moral! *If* only he returned to Salonika! *If* only he chose women who did not lead to his downfall! Thus, deep in the throes of sorrow, his soul spoke to me between sighs. My Uncle Leon was distraught over David, but I was afraid of him. I was afraid of the disease-bearing lice with which he was infested, and I was afraid of the demands he might one day make of me—demands that I, in all probability, could not satisfy.

From the time I met my uncle I began to fret about where I would live, but my uncle encouraged me to stay at the hotel. "There are many young people from Salonika here," he said, and indeed there were. I met a David Saporta, who had a room at the Atlas, and I moved in with him almost immediately. In David I had a friend and companion with whom I could share everything, and I was very lucky.

On his departure, my uncle left a suitcase with me, and in so doing he warned me never to give anything to his son, David. This was a matter of principle to

him, for its contents—a light summer suit, long winter underwear, and other miscellany—were not particularly valuable. Why these things were left behind
I do not know, for I never saw my uncle again.

My uncle and his wife and Sol went from Salonika to Auschwitz, and from there to the waiting gas
chambers. As for my cousin David, things went from
bad to worse. The crest of the wave he rode had been
high, and the trough was commensurately low. "Help
me," he cried one day when he came to see me. "I beg
you to help me!" Desperate beyond belief, devoid of
an iota of flamboyance, disheveled, full of lice, and
in a deplorable state, David lamented his condition.
He pleaded with me to give him something to wear,
but I had nothing, nothing at all, until I remembered
his father's suitcase. Poor David forgot to take the
lightweight suit, and wore his father's woolens in the
dead heat of summer. With the money I gave him—
money of my own—he made his way to Salonika,
where he was caught by the Germans and never seen
again. The epitome of eros had been consumed by voracious death.

While we were there, the owner of the Atlas never
took advantage of us through extortion or by any other
means—and all of us, mostly young people, lived
openly as Jews. We came and went, attended to our
affairs, developed memorable friendships, made love,
nurtured one another, and in effect became an ex-

tended family. The strands of normalcy were creating new cloth in Athens, but we could not forget that we had been separated from those we loved, and that we were involved in the serious business of seeing to their safe entry into Athens.

During this period my relationship with David Saporta consolidated and gained in strength and, at some point, we decided to leave the hotel. We rented a room together at a pensíon on Marnis Street, a street famous for its bordellos, far from the center of town and more or less in the fields, but when his sister Rachel and his brothers Joseph and Vital came to Athens, David moved in with them.

In those days Rachel had little respect for me, and from the time she had seen my girlfriend Calypso make a hasty retreat from the window of my first-floor apartment, she thought of me as a lowlife. We had been "busy," the landlady was at door, shouting and pounding on it to gain entry, and my girlfriend panicked. The incident, more comical than lurid, had made a definite impression.

One day, while I still lived with David, Rachel came by. The place was a shambles by female standards, and possibly by many other standards as well, but I was accustomed to this. The air in my room was oppressive, and Rachel—in an attempt to trace the source of an offending odor—aimlessly opened a drawer. Within it were a host of my putrid socks,

socks that—given the circumstances—elicited from her a tactful and understated, ladylike response. The impact of that discovery must have made it seem to her that I had gone from bad to worse now that I lived alone, and yet she cared; her sense of loyalty was very strong, and, despite her feelings, she had David come to see me and propose that I move in with them.

VI

Ni lluvia sin truelos,
ni parto sin dolores.

Neither rain without thunder,
nor childbirth without pain.

This radio broadcast was part of a German propaganda drive to encourage Greeks to "volunteer" for work in the Reich.

Dear Listeners, many of you have relatives, friends and acquaintances working in Germany, and you must often wonder about the kind of life they live there. Now listen:

It is afternoon. The workers are streaming from the workrooms and go laughing and talking towards the canteen. There are many thousands of workers. We see the Greek group over there. Let us go near them and ask them: 'Hey, boys!'

Worker: *Are you Greek?*

[*Babble of talk in Greek. Several Greek workers talking.*]

Announcer: *We want to know how you are getting on here.*

Worker: *It's now three months since I left Greece and came here. . . .*

Announcer: *How about the food?*

Worker: *Quite good. We get . . . bread, margarine, eggs, marmalade, macaroni. . . . We lack nothing.*

Announcer: *But look here, you seem to be getting much more than we get.*

Worker: *Yes, we do. Heavy workers get twice as much as others.*

Announcer: *And how is the work?*

Worker: *No hardship there, believe me . . .*

Announcer: *And are you taken care of otherwise?*

Worker: *As for care and welfare . . . they can't do enough for us. Let my chum here tell you what happened to him the other day.*

2nd Worker: *I had a toothache so I went to have my tooth extracted. The doctor extracted it and told me to go straight to bed. Me go to bed for a tooth I could have extracted with my bare fingers? So I went back to work laughing at the idea, and a little after, what do you think, a man came from the hospital and said he had orders to take me to bed. . . . So I went to the hospital for the night, I tell you, for a tooth I could have extracted with my bare fingers. Just think what they'll do if you are really taken ill.*

Announcer: *But boys, these things are not known at home. They would like to hear all about it.*

Workers: *Tell them we are fine, never better.*

British Archives
FO 898/153, April 28, 1943.

From Mark Mazower, *Inside Hitler's Greece*, 73–74.

The Saportas gathered together to take this photo prior to deportation. They did not know where they were going other than to "work in the East," and each wanted a memento in case they were separated. Ironically unaware of outside events or what awaited them, many made their own aprons for their supposed jobs. The Star of David evident here points to the fact that the photo was taken after the promulgation of the Racial Laws on February 6, 1943.

Right to left, front row: Sara Ackish, Rachel Saporta, Vital Saporta, Allegra Saporta (Vital's wife and Sara Ackish's sister), two unidentified women, and Joseph Saporta. Left to right, back row: Samuel and Esther Saporta. The others cannot be identified.

And so it was that fourteen of us shared a home: Rachel, David, Joseph, Vital and his wife, Allegra, an aunt and an uncle, two cousins, one of whom was crippled, the aunt's sister, her husband and two children, and I! Mr. and Mrs. Saporta and another sister, Georgette, who could not get out of Salonika in time, perished.

We were still under Italian occupation, and I now lived at Patmou #8. Across the street at Patmou #5 there lived a remarkable woman, a Mrs. Eleni Nikolaidis, and diagonally across from her backyard there lived another generous soul by the name of Yula Yazitzian—an Armenian woman who lived with her mother, or Ya Ya (grandmother), and three children. Two protectors were nearby.

The Gestapo were all over the place in little units here and there, and were on the lookout for male hostages. The Underground was active, and hand grenades were often smuggled into various households by hiding them in among the crates of charcoal, which were a commonplace in those days. For every German casualty or fatality, two, ten, twenty, fifty

The Yazitzians at a park in Athens.
Left to right: Garo, Azat, Yula,
and Agar. *1943.*

Yula Yazitzian's husband was in the carpet business and in
Persia during the war; after the war's end, he returned,
gathered his family together, and left for the Soviet
Union, given his faith in Communism. Before his departure, he promised to send a family photo from there to
Elia. At that time, they agreed upon a simple formula to
convey a particular message. If the family photo por-
trayed everyone standing, everything was fine; if everyone was seated in a chair, however, Elia could infer
that it was not. When the anticipated photo arrived,
everyone was sitting on the ground.

male Jews paid with their lives. These the Germans rounded up and either killed outright or sent to Haidari, and from there on to Auschwitz. The Gestapo's method was to post their trucks in an obscure corner, and to pounce upon and whisk away the unwary. This was our life, and these were the conditions under which we lived.

One day as David and I sorted through some wheat that lay on a tray propped upon our knees, idly extricating the tiny stones that turned up amid the grain, we heard a blast that sent the wheat flying into the air. A hand grenade that had been smuggled in among the charcoal by the Underground had detonated accidentally just three doors away from where we were and David, Joseph, and I, the only males at home, fled for our lives. We ran to the park, knowing full well that we could be rounded up by the Germans; at that time we did not know what the Italians might do if they caught us—but we were not eager to find out. The women remained where they were. For the time being, their situation was not as fragile as ours.

During this period, the newspapers under German control called for the conscription of Greek laborers according to certain specialties. Bulletins were posted everywhere throughout the city to this effect, but no one presented himself at the appointed time. Not long after this nonevent and display of resistance, the Communists and guerrilla groups got wind of the German plan to assault the Ministry of Labor in an attempt to forcibly confiscate their records for the selections. The Germans came with their tanks, accompanied by the Italians, but the Greek police were placed in the front lines—and what these men found surprised them. The area bordering the building swarmed with hundreds of thousands of people, I among them. The Greeks had come from everywhere, some from as far away as Salonika, and even the hospitals had been emptied to whatever degree was possible. Wounded soldiers on crutches, individuals in wheel chairs, and people from all walks of life were there in a show of solidarity and noncompliance. The Germans shot into the crowd and claimed their first casualties as the masses surged into an angry mob of protest.[1] A few bold, able-bodied Greeks jumped onto the tanks and the Greek police did little, but they did shoot into the ranks. The ensuing rampage pressed the Germans and Italians to retreat, and the unquenched mob now assaulted the Ministry in waves of undirected fury. It destroyed records, sent furniture flying through windows, and set the building afire. At last, amid the debris and flames, passions flickered and cooled. After the incident, the Germans approached the Archbishop. They sought to ease the state of unrest and in effect promised to not draft anyone. At this point, a few Greeks came forward to volunteer.

1. The sick and those on crutches and in wheel chairs were placed in the "front lines." The Greeks never dreamed that the Germans would fire upon the ill and infirm, but they were very much mistaken. These, then, were among the first casualties.

These and other incidents began to take their toll; our nerves were frayed, and we were on edge. The Spartan conditions under which we lived, fueled by our proximity to one another, allowed for no respite and exacerbated the tensions of war. We were draining our emotional resources at the very time we desperately needed to keep our wits about us. Still, as long as the Italians were the main military presence, we stayed where we were.

The unaccustomed wrangling, continual dissonance, and general state of affairs with fourteen of us under cumulative pressure continued to deteriorate our relationships with one another until the Italian surrender brought the entry of entire divisions of Germans into Athens. Now, more imperiled than ever before, we were forced to conclude that the time to separate had come. All ambiguity dissolved.

Those of us who had no children to think of and care for prepared to leave, but in order to do so we had to take two steps: the first was to contact the Underground—this was crucial because we did not know where to go—and the second was for each of us to convert about twenty liras worth of various gold coins into Greek drachmas. All of us had false ID's from our Salonika days, and these we had prepared for the purpose of passing various Italian or German controls; they had nothing to do with the issuance of ration cards, which we would not use in any case. (Because of our distinctive and telltale accents, clearly designating us as Jews, it was simply too risky.) Our direction would be toward the mountains of Free Greece, where we would be among peasants who would not barter for anything but the familiar drachma, and we had to be prepared. Each of us had worn a money belt filled with gold coins, the tender of survival in the city, but we now reversed course. We exchanged our gold and got a suitcase filled with the otherwise worthless drachma. When the time came, we would be ready to leave.

On the day our liaison contacted us, Rachel, Allegra, Vital, Joseph, David, and I set out with our suitcases to brave the hazards of flight. It was now the fall of 1943, and the Germans, who had entered Athens in strength, were tightening their stranglehold on the city and its Jews.

We met our contact at the designated rendezvous point, and there we found that he had gathered together three others who had chosen to flee. We now numbered nine: seven men and two women. Our coordinator's job was done; from now on, everything was up to us and the guerrillas entrusted with our care, armed men—mostly poorly educated villagers, some of whom were very rough—who had assumed the responsibility of escorting us to safety in an area that came under the jurisdiction of a Captain Orestes.

I no longer remember the names of all those we met on the arduous, week-long trek into the mountains, but I do remember that Sava, Dassa, and Dario Sham

were among them, that we got along very well, and
that we somehow managed to lift one another's spirits, laugh and sing, and sometimes even be downright
funny despite an unrelenting hunger.

Guerrilla bands streaked the mountainside like
schools of fish in streams of twenty or twenty-five
persons, clearly attesting to the fact that we were not
alone in our clamberings across the rocky terrain.
Once, along the way, we stopped on a hilltop in order
to rest—but not to eat, for we had no food. A shep-
herd tending his flock roamed nearby and our leader
approached him, beseeching him to give us a sheep—
but the man refused. After things went badly between them, our leader simply confiscated it. The
poor sheep was slaughtered, barbecued, and shared.
Rachel sat upon a rock and began to sing in order to
still our anxiety. Her voice rang out over the hills; it
floated into our hearts, and I never looked at her in
quite the same manner again. Our attitudes toward
one another were softening; deprivation and the common struggle out in the open, where we were exposed, subject to hunger, and tremblingly cold at
night, were silently knitting our destinies together.

One day we came across a girl who was lost; she
was a fugitive, and very frightened. Between sobs she
begged for protection. Far from gratifying her wish,
the guerrillas saw at once that she was a prostitute
and, inferring that as such she must have been a collaborator, decided to execute her. We, who were not

in the least convinced of the merit of their conclusion, pleaded for her life until we prevailed. "Don't do this," we urged. "After the war, there will be a tribunal; there will be justice, and she will be dealt with if she is guilty, but this is not the way." For a while the girl followed us—but one day she got lost, and we never saw her again.

Among us was an extraordinary young man who had committed to memory an enormous string of French words, the meanings of which were totally unknown to him. These words he would juxtapose at random to create a racing monologue of utter nonsense, a feat he could sustain for as long as fifteen minutes. Those of us who knew French roared at the images he sent colliding into the air to our delight and astonishment, but this was not the only aspect of his achievement—for he could do the same with Ladino, and could knowingly weave a fantastical tale rooted in absurdity. I remember that one such tale he called *"la banqueta y la almendra"* (The Little Bench and the Almond), but one would have had to have been there to appreciate the merriment he aroused and its effect upon us.

That first week we barely ate because we had encountered no one from whom we could buy any food. When we finally came to a village, things were not much better. The villagers grew their vegetables and made their own bread and wine; they, in fact, went to Thivas, a town some twenty miles away, when they needed one staple or another. Still, they were very kind and very quick to relieve our plight with an onion here, an eggplant or zucchini there, a tomato, or a few grapes—and all this out of the goodness of their hearts, for they would not accept any of the drachmas we had brought along.

Despite sporadic acts of kindness, we were starving. Dario pretended to be a wine merchant and went from villager to villager to "sample" the grapes; the vines were full, and his conscience was clear. "I don't want to die of hunger," he said to us, and he did not. He awakened early each morning, scanned the horizon to check the chimneys from which smoke swirled into the air, and then decided where to go for breakfast. At the very least, on that day he would have freshly baked bread to eat. The rest of us were too reserved to do as he did; hungry as we were, we could not beg. For the most part we were biding our time, but there were occasions when desperation drove us to steal from the fields.

Now, where were we?

Our escorts had seen us safely to an area composed of five villages and known as Dervanohoria, where we were expected. A meeting of welcome had been called and Captain Orestes, an officer in the army, greeted us. His jurisdiction covered each of the five villages, and we could opt to live in any one of them. The villages themselves formed a kind of square, with a village at each corner and one at the center—and be-

cause we reasoned that the central village was protected by the other four, we decided to stay there.
Before long, it was possible to assess that the partisans
mainly consisted of the males living in each of the villages. They were basically illiterate, fanatical types,
professing to be Communists. In reality, however,
they knew little or nothing of the precepts of Communism, and were more or less products of the fer-
ment of the times—men who had embraced a symbol
around which they could unite.

We rented an unattached barn that was about 14' x
14' in size, and all nine of us stayed in it. We had a
fireplace and a window, but no toilet and no water.
The walls were finished, but the floors were made of
cement, and we had nothing warm to wear against
the cold. We slept on the floor, chilled to the bone
without blankets, and we relieved ourselves in the
fields. There was no possibility to bathe, and no such
amenity as toilet paper. If we could, we used leaves,
but we often used the money—which gave rise to
many jokes.

From the outset we had wanted to bear arms, but
according to Orestes the partisans did not have
enough weapons to share with us. On the one hand
we were relieved because the taking of life was repug-
nant to us; on the other hand we were rueful because
many of us had served in the Greek Army, and we very
much wanted to defend ourselves and our homeland.

One day an alarm spread through the village. As

many as one hundred Germans had been seen scouting through the woods, and the news electrified us into action—or rather, a state of panic. Rumors spread and speculation of a traitor among the Greeks ran high, but what were we to do? A debate arose. The partisans wanted to kill the Germans and we, who had shared in the general discussions, were not so sure. "If you kill them, what do you think will happen?" We tried to urge Orestes to think of the consequences. "The others will look for these men," we said. "They cannot just 'disappear': they have to be accounted for. They must report back—and if they don't, a search party will set out to find them. The Germans will come here in force; they will come with their tanks and artillery, demolish everything, and kill everyone."

We thought it best not to offer too much resistance, knowing full well that what we were suggesting had its risks. "Let them find a sleepy little village if they chance upon us," we advised, but not even we were convinced. We knew perfectly well that only women and children were the mainstay of the village, for all able men bore arms and patrolled the villages to keep them secure. Ultimately, the partisans set out in the absence of a solid solution. They ambushed and killed the Germans, and we were now more apprehensive than ever. We were in a no-win situation, precisely because the aspect of normalcy was missing.

Our hunger mounted day by day, and we decided to send someone from within our group to Thivas for food. We hired a Greek villager, who knew many secret byways and whom we paid very handsomely, to accompany him. Seven names went into a hat, and Sava was chosen by lot. Because of the risks, it was unthinkable to send either Rachel or Allegra—and neither name was cast.

Sava and the Greek set out on two mules. By evening of the same day, we who had remained behind sat out of doors in the crisp night air. It was beautiful in the moonlight, and we began to dream of the goods that might never come. We dreamed of what we would eat and how we would cook it, and we lathered our hunger into a frenzy of desire. Very late the next night, the men arrived. They had been successful—but because of the hour, they had first stored everything in the stable. The feast we had salivated for did not materialize that night or ever as it turned out, but we were happy because Sava was safe and had returned to us.

Our joy lasted for perhaps two hours, and then we fell asleep. At four o'clock that same morning, we were awakened by a terrible din. The women of the village were in a panic. They pounded on doors, and they ran and screamed: "The Germans are here! The Germans are here!" Nowhere was an able man to be seen; every man was out, either fighting or on patrol. We were being routed within a day of the attack on the Germans.

We left everything and fled as we were, neither knowing where we were going nor where the Germans were. The nine of us and the village women, followed by the cows and sheep they habitually tended, ran toward and climbed the mountains, and in the scramble to distance ourselves, Rachel lost a shoe. We broke the heel of the other shoe to make it easier on her and kept going, but I ran barefoot over the hills; my shoes were too tight to do otherwise. In the midst of flight and chaos, and amid screams and shots, a baby was born.

On the evening of the next day we arrived at an olive orchard. It soon would be dark, and a cold mist promised to envelop us. We heard the howling of wolves, and saw the glow of their eyes. Three of us climbed a tree, and with all our strength battered a limb with our bodies in order to break it. When we succeeded, we set it afire to ward off the wolves. Luckily, the limb was oily and the tree perhaps a little old, for it burned well. In all this, Vital was the most courageous of us all. The rest of us were bound up in our fears. If we did not start a fire, we feared the wolves; if we did, we feared the Germans. Vital insisted on the fire, and that night I slept between Rachel and Allegra in order to keep warm. As we dozed, others kept watch. It had been an eventful day, an epic day of Herculean effort, raw survival, and monstrous death. Vital had scrambled about and found a variety of berries we knew nothing of but nevertheless ate, and we had run across instances where captured Germans had been beheaded in a repulsive manner with shards of glass. The villagers, all of whom were partisans, had gone wild, and Orestes could not control them.

The following morning we saw a village somewhere in the distance; it was one of the five under Orestes' jurisdiction, and we went there. There were no Germans in sight. We stood on a hilltop and scanned the horizon. Four of the villages had been burned, and the fate of this one could not be in doubt. We had to leave—and this time, nothing short of a miracle could save us. At last we came to a spot we thought was deserted and, incredibly, we sat in an empty café to plan our next move. Before long, we noticed a man doing something that was perfectly normal. Stunned for a moment, we watched as he loaded charcoal onto a run-down truck—and then we approached him. "Where are you going?" we asked, and he replied: "To Athens." The miracle we needed was unfolding before our very eyes. "Can we hide?" we asked again, and he said: "Get in. I'll take you to Athens."

We hid among the coal and passed many controls without incident—and by evening of the same day we arrived in Athens, black with coal dust from head to toe. In all, we had been gone about four weeks.

VII

*Con paciencia, y de la yerba
se hace seda.*

With patience, even grass can
be made into silk.

It was late at night, and we were utterly unrecognizable as we made our way, in defiance of the curfew, to Kiria Maria.[1] Overcome with shock at our appearance, she tried to shut us out after having opened the door. "Mme. Maria, it's me, Elia! Open the door! Please!" I had screamed in desperation, and now she knew me. Between tears and hugs, we entered. She fed us and allowed us to wash, and on that night six of us—Rachel and Allegra, David, Joseph, Vital and I—slept in her home.[2] The next morning we contacted Mrs. Nikolaidis at Patmou #5 through an intermediary, and Vital left with Allegra for Thivas, where they had many friends and Vital could hope to work.[3] It was a necessity to separate, and Patmou #8 never crossed our minds.

Through our contact with Mrs. Nikolaidis, David, Joseph, Rachel, and I found asylum in the home of her neighbor Yula Yazitzian, a woman who had in the past

1. *Kiria:* a mode of address equivalent to *Madame*, denoting respect. Kiria Maria lived in the area of Sepolia and was Elia's uncle's neighbor. She knew the family. Joseph Errera, his wife Mary, with his children and Tanasaki, a nephew, had stayed with her for some months before they moved to Loutraki.

2. When the alarm came that the Germans had penetrated the village, these six clung together tenaciously; the other three, who were part of the original nine to have fled to the mountains, scattered. Some are known to have survived.

3. Thivas was known as a cotton and textile center.

4. She faithfully set the table for their lunch and dinner each day, a gesture both simple and replete with regard, but because of the high cost of electricity they ate their dinner early and by candlelight.

opened her heart to us in many ways.[4] We now shared adjacent backyards with Patmou #5, as well as with the Carassos and Benvenistes—all of whom were related to the Saportas and from whom we had parted only four weeks earlier. We signaled to one another across the distance that separated us, but we did not visit. Sometimes, though, when we were crazy enough, we shouted to one another from across the way.

The Yazitzians lived in the basement apartment of a three-story building, which they entered from the side of the house. The apartment's barred windows— some of which faced the main street—were at ground level, so that it was always possible to see the feet and part of the legs of passersby. One day, as we looked out the window, we were confronted with the ill-boding sight of a German soldier's boots. Whoever was out there paced back and forth, and had to be on guard duty. To and fro went the boots for hours on end, until we were utterly petrified. At long last a military vehicle pulled to the curb, and more boots were to be seen. "They have come for us," we cried among ourselves, but Mrs. Yazitzian remained steadfast and said nothing. Before long the boots entered by the front door, and later on we learned that the Germans had come for an Italian spy for the Allies.

Yula Yazitzian's character never faltered, and yet

her life and the lives of her children and mother were at stake and in her hands at the precipitation of a moment. Clearly, our good fortune rested in the fact that both Yula and Eleni Nikolaidis had entered our lives.

From everything she said one would not doubt for a moment that Mrs. Nikolaidis was unconsciously anti-Semitic; from everything she did, however, she proved herself a woman of incomparable compassion. She brought food and sweets to us, gave us daily accounts of the news on BBC—which she monitored on her clandestine radio—helped us in every way, and invited Rachel and me to dinner frequently in the full knowledge of her husband, who was an angel. "The only reward I want," she once said to me, "is for you to celebrate your engagement in my home." She was capable of the most unbelievable expressions of love to all, but for Rachel there was a special feeling; she accepted her like a daughter. To us ordinary mortals perhaps she was an enigma, but more likely than not she was a saint unaware of her qualities.

We lived with danger every day, and the pressure was unrelenting. Everything was imperative, everything seemed to happen simultaneously. The negotiations and transactions in gold coin had to go on; these were not the woods. The woolen goods in hidden storehouses could not be neglected, and neither could the bulging money belt and the greed it incited. These matters had to be dealt with. The moves, emergencies, urgencies of youth, and quest for food—despite Mrs. Nikolaidis's generosity—pressed upon us; the need for privacy—a place to think, plan, absorb horror and recover, at least for the moment, all these clamored for attention. The telephone calls—appointments duly made—the letters and guarded talk, the couriers, fatigue, money drain, risks and fatal mistakes, and the "new" problem, the nascent collaborators—who reported the whereabouts of the Jews in hiding—all these arose with explosive force.5

5. Albala (from Salonika), Recanati (from Salonika and then operative in Athens), and Hasson (a traitor from Salonika), in particular.

The house by the sea was enveloped in the mists of history. An alien tide was sweeping away those who lived in or loved it, and wave upon successive wave pounded to extinction tens of thousands more. Everything that happened from 1941 to 1943, no matter how loving or valiant the response, had been the prelude to disaster.

VIII

*Il lobo y la oveja vienen
en una conseja.*

The wolf and sheep appear
in the same story.

Joseph and Mary and the children left Athens when the Italians capitulated, and went to Loutraki on the strength of Joseph's connections. Seemingly, he had made a sound choice; a choice that had taken into consideration the advantages of being near Athens, but not so near that the children had to be overly careful while at play. The exercise of caution in this respect was crucial and not a mere parental indulgence, for the children spoke differently from one another— and this was not a matter to be overlooked. Eli and Marcel, Joseph and Mary's biological children, could be identified readily as Jews because their Greek was accented by Ladino, Italian, and French inflections, but Tanasaki, who had been raised among Greeks in the town of Xanthi, approximately three hundred miles northeast of Salonika and on the way to Turkey, and had gone to a Greek school, spoke with an accent that was indiscernible from that of other Greeks. Unless made to disrobe—for there was always the tell-tale circumcision to give one away—Tanasaki enjoyed a certain immunity none of the others could claim.

The unpredictable element that arose at Loutraki had to do with the landlord's expressed attraction for

Mary. Given the unwanted attention and circumstances, Mary's rejection was fraught with danger. All
one's tact, intelligence, and capacity for fine tuning—
and good, old-fashioned luck—would have to be
called into play. Averting disaster in this situation was
not going to be easy simply because my uncle had
made up his mind to move.

Joseph's note to me sent me spinning into a flurry
of activity. My friends made inquiries of others here
and there and I scoured the town, constantly on the
move, ready to finalize plans should the right place
present itself. Meanwhile, ever sensing the
potential prey, Recanati, the collaborator,[1]
approached Rachel's brother Vital. "Where
is Elia?" he at first asked, but then he probed
further: "He has a lot of money, hasn't he?"
"I have ways of finding out where he is,"
Vital responded, but he knew very well
where I was and he came to see me. "Get out
of here," he warned. "They're looking for
you."[2]

In time I found a villa outside of Athens.
It was at the *Terma,* or end of the trolley line,
out in the fields, and near a ravine filled with
brush—a perfect hideout, bounded by an
ivy-covered iron fence. If we were out of
doors we would have to whisper, I thought,
but we would not be seen.

The villa had six steps leading to a well-

1. Recanati, who knew
hosts of Sephardim from
his Salonika days, con-
tinued to collude with
the Germans when in
Athens. He used his fa-
miliarity with the commu-
nity to ferret out and report those who were
known to him and oth-
erwise safe in hiding.
What drove him to such
lengths as to report mere
children and entire fami-
lies, sometimes accom-
panying the Germans
on their roundup, can-
not be fathomed.

2. The Germans. An
inference based upon
Recanati's known or
suspected collusion.

kept apartment in the basement, which was occupied by the owner and his wife, a childless couple. The main floor had four bedrooms—all of them large; all of them furnished—and all windows bore heavy burgundy velvet drapes, an added advantage or safeguard. Above the main floor was a terrace. The owner, who knew we were Jews and understood the situation we were in, was a fair man; he would treat us justly, and I felt comfortable reporting my findings to Joseph.

Deeply troubled by the duration of the war, dwindling funds, and the impossibility of knowing how long everyone would have to remain underground, Joseph determined to rent the villa as long as he could share its costs with the family of a business associate. I knew these people, but I did not know them well. "This is a mistake," I warned, thinking of our safety and not their character, but by now Joseph was too worried by the economics of survival to heed my plea.

My reasoning and reluctance to involve others was sensible, but it did not prevail. It could not, for Joseph's every argument carried greater merit in the real world of our increasingly uncertain existence. It was therefore decided that the Mishulams were to share the villa with us, and we resolved to do our best before the agreement was sealed.

I moved into the villa and had a bedroom of my own; Joseph, Mary, and their children were in another bedroom, with Tanasaki in still another. The

Mishulam family, which consisted of a husband and wife, son and daughter, occupied the fourth room. The girl, about sixteen, was an astonishingly ethereal beauty, breathtaking to behold, so that once one had seen her, she could not be forgotten. It was now either late 1943 or early 1944.

During the eight to ten months we lived in the villa we did not feel the need to articulate any special house rules. When it was hot we spent a good part of the day in the front yard, where we had to be very quiet. We played cards, read newspapers loaned to us by our landlord, and devised certain divertissements with which to occupy ourselves. One of these was to pitch handsful of cucumbers into the well in order to cool them off, and then later to fish them out with a bucket. When it was not hot, our activities changed accordingly.

Theoretically, none but Tanasaki was to leave the grounds. He was "The Greek" among us, the "safe one" no one would take to be a Jew, the one with many friends "on the outside." He was also a manly boy of eleven; a person in whom much trust had been placed and to whom great responsibility fell. We had not applied for our ration cards in order to keep as low a profile as possible, and so we had to rely upon him in many ways. He bought our cucumbers and tomatoes, and went to the mill to have our grain ground into flour; he brought our dough to the communal oven, and returned with our bread after it had been baked.

Our intention to remain as cloistered as possible, so logically arrived at in theory, was not realized. I still had responsibilities to discharge that were vitally connected with our survival, and I dreadfully missed David and Rachel.

David continued to be my good friend and confidant, and Rachel and I were becoming closer. Sometimes we met at a quarry, where we flirted with one another, and sometimes I went there alone to collect my thoughts. I was experienced and adept at what I had to do and I did not endanger anyone, but complications had arisen with regard to the Mishulams—complications that troubled me more than words can express.

The Mishulams were poor and took risks, just as we did, in order to survive. One such risk involved the stubborn refusal to forgo the use of ration cards, which clearly identified them as Jews by virtue of their surname, and the other was the fateful error of sending their unforgettably beautiful daughter into town. The girl's accent was not a problem, and her Greek was flawless. "It's wrong," I complained to my uncle. "What you are doing is wrong! How much can you save?" Clearly arguing for them to stop or face removal, I cried: "Someday, something is going to happen! Can't you see that she is buying bread?" *"Como que le diga?"* ("How can I tell her?") My uncle was very disturbed. How could he say this or anything like it? "Then give them the bread yourself," I urged.

"Give them bread, so that she doesn't go beyond the gates of the house!" But my poor uncle could not take this step either. The Mishulams would be hurt. They had pride, and it would shame them to accept charity.

The result of all this sensitivity was that the poor girl was detected on two occasions. The first time, she returned badly shaken and in tears; the second time, it seems she could have evaded detection—but I was not there and I did not get the full story.

As long as I live I will never forget the day of August 2, 1944, for on that day the Mishulam girl went to the bakery for the last time. On that day too, Tanasaki, who had been returning from the flour mill, was captured by the Germans. His friends greeted him wildly,[3] giving him news of events at the villa—news that attracted the Germans, connected him irrevocably to the Erreras, and engulfed him in the tragic sweep of the roundup then in place.[4]

The night before these events had been difficult for me. A recurring sense of impending dread kept me from sleeping so that by morning my anxiety had mounted intolerably, rendering me speechless. "Go to the Saportas. Relax with your friends. You need a break," my uncle said, and I took his advice. I went to Patmou #8, fully intending to return much earlier than I eventually did.

3. The children had yelled "Tanasaki! Tanasaki!" and had run to him dramatically enough to alert the Germans. Elia learned of this later from the landlord, who saw it happen.

4. Since the nineteenth and last transport out of Salonika removed all Jews from the city on August 18, 1943, this roundup signaled the end of the entire family. No one knew about or suspected genocide at this time.

Tanasaki Ezrati, right, helping two unidentified
vendors prior to his capture along with
the Erreras and the Mishulams.
Athens, 1944.

My visit with the Saportas lasted longer than expected due to an unpredictably strange occurrence
that defies both nature and all reason, and to this day
remains utterly unfathomable. "Eat with us," said the
Saportas. "We have some string beans." Now, string
beans are not a complicated affair and do not take long
to cook, but these remained hard as stone after three
long hours of engaging our curiosity. Why they never
cooked I will never know, but I missed the roundup
that day by a hair's breadth.

Immediately upon my return from the Saportas I
noticed that something was not right. The windows
and doors of the villa were open, but we were always
careful about this, and they were never open before.
(It is strange and contradictory but true that we tried
to give no outward sign of our existence at the same
time that the Mishulam girl had been a walking bea-
con that could and did lead the Germans to the door.)
What I had not seen was the long, black car parked
nearby. That was very clever of the Germans.

I walked into the house and peered into the kitchen. Two Germans in short pants were there. They
did not see me but the landlord did, and he pushed
me out of the way. "Get out of here," he warned when
we were outside, but I was frantic and cried: "I have
money! I can bribe them!" "Get out of here, or they'll
catch you too," he insisted. My money belt was full of
gold and I wanted to go back into the house, but he

would not let me do this. The Germans had already been in my bedroom. They had seen my pajamas lying on the bed just as I had left them, and for the time being they had accepted the landlord's story explaining them away.

I fled to the quarry and sat on a rock, my emotions in a rampage. I felt a profound sadness—what had happened was no joke—and yet I was curiously at peace. I was relieved. Now that everyone was gone, I did not have to fight any more. I had worried about everyone and everything, and it had been torture to me, but now I thought that whatever could happen had happened. I believed that the worst was over, and that everybody would return. That was the first rush. The second rush was fear. They will beat my uncle, I thought, and he will tell them where I have been.

A momentary paralysis seized me, and then I began to move. I ran to the Saportas.[5] I told them what I knew and what I was afraid of—never dreaming of the actual reality—and then an incredible thing happened. With the exception of the Carassos—an aunt and an uncle, their son and crippled daughter—and the four Benvenistes, six of us took flight. We bolted just as we were. Those who remained behind never left Patmou #8, and never came to any harm.

5. Because the Carassos and the Benvenistes were two branches of the Saporta family, Elia continually refers to them as "the Saportas."

IX

Coro, coro, en un lugar mi topo.

I run and run and find myself
in one place.

Before leaving, David, Joe, Rachel, and I decided to separate and meet at a predetermined location amid the trees in Alsos Park, a distance of some two or three miles from where we were. I remember clearly that it was a hot and humid day.

All of us arrived safely at the rendezvous point and, little by little, we began to think of what to do. Vital and his wife, who were in Thivas on a business trip, were staying with friends; they went back and forth quite often, and often brought those at either end what news they could.[1] It was imper-ative to notify them of what had happened and to warn them to stay where they were. We therefore went to an office in Athens, where we met with a merchant with whom Vital worked, a man of Greek Orthodox background who agreed to be our intermediary. He needed time to work things out and we lived in the park for two days, trying to make the best of the situation. During the night we huddled together under the arms of a tree, in terror of being caught after curfew; during the day, we moved about and tried to stay

1. Vital, trying to make a living, went back and forth between Thivas, a small town that was a part of Free Greece, and Athens.

calm. Meanwhile I procured food for us with my gold coins, but we all hid money in our belts, and it was a very common thing to do.

At the end of two days the merchant, who may or may not have been in the Underground, recommended a temporary refuge for us in an espionage center that outwardly operated as a "house of entertainment" for the elite among the German officers. It was a big, two-story house, and it was furnished very well.

The "madam" expected us and immediately ushered us into a room; she explained that very little in the way of security was available to us and then left. The Germans came in and out. We heard their partying, and we were very frightened.

For two days and two nights we stayed in this house, not daring to speak unless it was absolutely necessary. We slept in one room, ate, and had facilities available to us, but we dared not shower or wash our clothes, which were filthy. At the end of the two days, the merchant brought word from Vital. He had a friend who would take us in. The only individual with whom we had had contact—the woman who received us—would accept no money from us in appreciation, and we now went from one precarious situation to another.[2]

Our next stop was to the roof of a six-

2. It was generally felt that this woman was a very fine person, and it is known that she was a society woman. According to some accounts, she had short-wave access to the Allies from the house; according to other accounts, she conveyed what she learned directly to the English and Greek spies who worked for the Allies and were known to be in Athens.

story building in town where a one-room shack—really a converted tool shed—awaited us. It had a toilet and sink, which we were to share with a thirty-five-year-old single man who worked there making wallets, so that the machine with which he stitched the leather was also in the "apartment." This man, whom we called "the wallet man," was Vital's boss and well aware of the danger he incurred; he was the Bohemian type and exceptionally good natured, despite the fact that the Germans had stripped him of his leather goods business. We had a lot of fun with him, for he was a cheerful man, but that did not prevent us from being frightened out of our wits.

The sun beat down on us, and the humidity oppressed us. We could not breathe in the shed by day, and there was too little room for us to sleep in it by night. We had but one recourse—to sleep in the open air, and that was problematic. Immediately next door—with not so much as an inch between them—was another six-story building, a hotel, filled with Germans.[3] They too had been overcome by the heat and had hit upon the same idea—so there we were, back-to-back, at the same level, totally at the mercy of chance. We saw one another and heard one another, and the Germans—who were drunk quite often—could have reached us with ease at any time.

After about two weeks, we began to think

3. It was as if attached and part of the same building. This was not unusual; other buildings were similarly attached.

of returning to Patmou #8. Our physical discomfort goaded us and our predicament tempted fate, but other factors arose to encourage us at this time. Along with the food he somehow managed to secure for us, the wallet man brought us a wealth of news and a host of newspapers put out by the underground press. *"Tous fagame!"* He related the joyful news: "We 'ate' them! We 'destroyed' them!" he cried. "Do you know something? The Allies are 'over there' already, and pretty soon they'll be over here!"

One day in mid-August, the four of us walked out of the building for the first time. We were two miles away from Patmou #8, and we went there on foot, all of us together. It was still light out, and we arrived before the curfew hour.

We knocked on the door. Someone peeked through the shutters and ushered us in. We were home, and there was no longer any reason to hide. The tide had changed. For the first time there was normalcy, and some kind of peace in the house. We now knew we were going to make it. Our neighbors protected us, and no one bothered us. The Germans were losing the war. They did not have the same power, and they were no longer sure of themselves. We watched them as they walked. Around and around they twirled as they made their way through town, trying to avoid being shot in the back.

Soon the bombings began. The English soared overhead and hundreds of planes covered the sky. Strategic facilities were being blown to bits, the supply of war material available to the Germans was being cut off, and we Greeks, Jew and non-Jew alike, saw the sight and applauded the spectacle. We were on the rooftops, and we were not afraid.

X

In tiempo de hambrera
no hay mal pan.

In a time of hunger, no bread is bad.

After the liberation some time in the fall of 1944, the six of us who had stuck together through thick and thin decided to look for a place of our own in which to live. The circumstances that had required the fourteen of us to stay at Patmou #8 no longer applied, and we set about our task with diligence. Rentals were difficult to locate and our job was not easy, but in time we found a three-bedroom apartment—the landlord of which demanded a huge sum as a "goodwill offering," or basic extortion. Given the circumstances, we tried hard to get the money.

I focused on reclaiming the stored woolen goods my uncle had arranged safekeeping for, but I met with little success or outright opposition. The crates full of bolts of fabric were for the most part denied me. Some claimed I never gave them anything; others threatened to have fascist thugs beat and kill me if I ever mentioned the subject again; still others coolly presented me with bogus receipts and claimed that the Nazis had taken the goods; and a few returned a small amount of little value. Most of the goods had been stolen, and in their absence I saw a weight of evidence signifying how well the merchants had fared from the time I had built the clandestine storehouses on their properties and stocked them with Joseph's woolens. In one instance, I felt very bad. I cursed the individual who had lied to me. "God *knows* what happened!" I cried. "If I am wrong, something terrible will happen to me, but if you are wrong, it will happen to you!" Within six months he died of tuberculosis, and I was horrified by my utterance ...

Eventually we managed to move into the apartment, which was spacious and consisted of three bedrooms, two living rooms, a dining room, kitchen, single bathroom, and a maid's room. It was absolutely empty, but we were full of hope. Little by little we would be able to get the essentials, and we did not give in to despair.

The winter of 1944 was bitterly cold and the hope that filled our hearts upon liberation was now cast down. The outbreak of a Communist revolution was in full force; the guerrillas had left their outposts in the mountainsides and had embarked upon an attempt to take over the country. The ensuing skirmishes, which claimed many lives, left little room for rejoicing.

The revolution was scarcely an abstraction. Every street was a battlefield and each rooftop was manned by machine gunners; they shot at everything that moved, and once more we were locked within the house. We had little to eat, and that little consisted of a few packets of worm-infested, dehydrated soup. When we boiled the contents the worms rose to the surface, and when we removed the worms we ate what remained. We were very hungry.

During this period, four or five acquaintances who had survived the concentration camps returned and came to live with us. They had no one and nowhere to go, and we took them in. While they searched for anyone known to them and tried to get settled, they used one of the living rooms as a sitting area and slept on the floor. Whenever they came, Rachel added water to the dehydrated soup. *"Fazi fijos,"* make children, she said, and we understood her meaning. She had commanded the water to multiply the soup.

As the first of the survivors left, others came. And so it was. They came and went, and we never turned anyone away. The stories they shared shocked us, and we began to fear for our families. At last, even though we knew nothing specific, we understood that we would never see our loved ones again.

One day a group of guerrillas came to our door, asking for me. They had heard I had goods in the house, which they needed. Vital, who had seen them coming from a window, greeted them at the door with a cane in hand; he had been wounded in the war with Albania and had a slight knee problem. "Comrades, you are mistaken," he said. "I live here, and you have wrong information. Please," he went on, "don't add more grief to my existence. I am an invalid." Strangely enough, they apologized: "Sorry, brother. It was a mistake."

Another day, we learned that the Jewish Agency was distributing food through the Red Cross. David and I decided to apply—for our plight was desperate—but the guerrillas were out in force. They shot at us from the time we left the house, and we dodged bullets the entire way. When we arrived, we were asked to prove we were Jews. "Are you circumcised?" they stammered, but the unfamiliar word had been mutilated sorely and faltered on the tongue. We helped them pronounce it and said: "Yes." Our reply seemed sufficient; no demonstration of fact was required of us, and on that day we went home with flour, beans, rice, and other staples. Every inch of the way back was fraught with danger, however, and it was with a great deal of luck that we evaded the bullets flying at us from all directions. We were utterly relieved to be alive, and that night we were at last able to cook and savor a decent meal with the supplies we had obtained and the utensils our neighbors had been kind enough to give us.

XI

Lloran cuerpos, enriba vestidos.

Within our clothes, our bodies cry.

One morning we awakened to no noise. Everything was still, and it frightened us. We peeked through the shutters. The streets were deserted. Little by little, we dared to venture into the open. At first there was caution; then there was surprise and joy, and then there was screaming. "They are gone! The English are here!" The eerie calm had been broken, and everyone ran to the center of town. The English were parading, and emotions ran high. For the second time, we had been liberated: once from the Germans, and once from the Communists.

From this point on, we tried to normalize our lives. We gathered together a few pieces of furniture and began to introduce a little comfort into our existence. More importantly, Rachel and I decided to marry. We became engaged and, true to her expressed wish years earlier, Mrs. Nikolaidis helped us celebrate the event in her home.

I should have been happy, but how could I be? My sights were on Salonika. The many unanswered questions about my family divided my soul and gave me no peace. I went to the quarry, and there I sat in solitude, brooding upon a rock. I was engaged, but I did not want to marry; I was close to those I loved, but I felt empty. The wars were over, but I had lost my mooring. The future loomed before me like that of a black hole, and I stepped into it as one who falls into an abyss.

Rachel urged me to return to Salonika. "Finish with that," she cried. "Settle it." It was clear to her that as long as I was torn by doubt or driven by ghosts, we would not be able to get on with our lives. She herself had no thought of leaving. She had looked into the mirror of reality and had seen a reflection of stark truth. Nothing and no one awaited her in Salonika, and no thought or hope of a miracle prompted her to leave Athens. Her parents and sister were dead; the life and world she knew were gone. She could not bear more than that.

I prepared to leave, along with several others. Jacques Matarasso, Albert Nissim's girlfriend Ida, Tia Mazaltov Nefoussi, her daughter Frida, and I rented an ill-fated truck and off we went, little realizing the adventures in store for us. Mishap after mishap detained us and prolonged the trip, but when an axle broke by a remote village, our journey came to a standstill. Parts had to be sent for, and for days on end we stayed at a modest hotel.

Our trip from Athens to Salonika had taken a long time; it had imposed an inadvertent moratorium upon us, and had deferred the impending confrontation with the residues of our fractured lives.

XII

*Pesa el oro, pesa el plomo, pesa
el hombre mas que todo.*

Weigh the gold, weigh the lead,
weigh the man most of all.

I rented a room in a cheap hotel and tried to learn what I could, but I did not feel well and within a week or so of my arrival I became quite ill. I was diagnosed as having pneumonia and a Dr. Alalouf, who had survived Auschwitz, took care of me.

As soon as I was able to, I got in touch with Leon Guilidi and his bride, Bertha, whom we called "Angel." They were the Saportas' friends and they were very good to me; they were, in fact, very good to many of us who had been in hiding, and their place became our refuge. No matter what we did by day, no matter what we encountered, we visited the Guilidis every night. There we were young; there we flirted and sought new constructs, and there we healed the wounds that lacerated us in broad daylight.[1]

The Guilidis owned a building several stories high that housed a popular bar on its first floor; here, as we entered, the ambience lifted the spirits, but in the apartment we were at home. Once within those walls a certain abandonment or loosening of restraints

1. Two Greek girls and seven or eight Jewish girls stayed with the Guilidis; they were in a terrible mental state and related to one another as family. They all dined together and sometimes went dancing or rowboating. Leon and Elia were generally the only males in the household, and Elia had a crush on Angel, who was very beautiful. They did not have an affair; the regenerative sparks were in relief to a tragic background, a series of events one does not fully recover from.

Top, left: The Guilidis and friends. Leon
is pointing and Berta (Angel) is to his
right. Top, right: Berta, Vital Saporta
(Rachel's brother), and a friend at the
window of the Guilidi apartment.
Bottom: Leon Guilidi in an unguarded
moment, gaiety unmasked.
Salonika, 1945.

typified Leon, but whether this stemmed from his true character or a facade, a reaction to the war or a release from the world we knew, I do not know. There were no parents, no children, no nieces or nephews, and no elder sisters or brothers before whom to be reticent.

Soon after my recovery, I worked alongside other Jews in an effort to help the few displaced persons liberated from the camps who had trickled in. Most of them were girls, all of whom were both bereft and glad to be alive. These were very painful, bittersweet days. "It won't stay this way forever"; "I can't make my life with dead people"; "If I don't get a grip on myself, I'll be gone too." This is what I heard them say. In so doing, they expressed what I felt. The wounded were helping the wounded.

Once in a while, I got news of one or another of the concentration camp survivors we had taken in while I was still in Athens. One settled somewhere in Greece and another, a man who once had worked for my uncle Joseph, made his way to Palestine. Still another I saw in Salonika; this was Haim, who had lost a leg— an emaciated being who dreamed aloud of how he yearned to open a café of his own. He lamented that he had nothing with which to make a start, and then prevailed upon me to loan him the money.

I had been eking out an existence by pleading for the return of Joseph's woolens and sometimes getting a moth-infested bolt or two here and there, and I had the gold bracelet my father had entrusted to my friend, the Italian soldier I had hoped could bring my sister Sol back with him from Salonika. This bracelet I painstakingly chipped away at or cut when I was most desperate. "Here," I used to say to one of Mrs. Yazitzian's sons. "Take this. Convert it. Bring some salami into the house." He never failed, and this is how it had been in the recent past. I still had a part of my mother's bracelet left and a little to get by on. I could not refuse him, and I thought I could manage.

Haim realized his dream. He opened a café at a busy intersection near a bus stop, and people came and went. They ordered coffee and had cake. They had a little of this and that, and they chatted or played backgammon until the oppressive heat of midday gave way. He was happy; he was successful; and he knew the rudiments of survival. He did not proffer the money I had advanced, and I never saw it. I went to the café, visited with him and others, and let it pass. It was but one of the many difficult truths I had to absorb while in Salonika, and it was not the worst.

When the few Jews from Salonika who survived the camps returned, I began to get news of my family. One told me that my father and brother had been part of a slave labor detail assigned to the construction of roofs, and that the work had been too difficult for my father. Through him I learned that my father had been gassed and my brother had died of typhus. Someone else told me that Tanasaki's little sister, whom my par-

Right to left: Haim, Elia, another friend, who tried to court Rachel in Elia's absence from Athens, Leon Guilidi, and two unidentified friends.
Salonika, 1945.

ents had adopted, had been thrown into a pit and burned alive, and that my mother and sister had been gassed immediately on arrival at Auschwitz. Another gave me a message from Guillaume. "Don't forget the money in Switzerland," he had said—but what money? Which account? And where? From the little I learned, I gleaned the awesome rest; I could infer what had happened to those I would never see again.

From the time I recovered from pneumonia I was making discoveries of my own, salvaging what I could, and sometimes unaccountably rejecting the custodianship of other items that were rescued by that rarest of all beings—the uncorrupted person; the friend or neighbor who did not exploit the misfortunes of others.

I now can see that on the unconscious level I was cautious in retracing the steps of the past. I began by going to Guillaume's place. There I found that Mme. Boyer, a simple woman quick to take advantage of circumstance, was in control. I could salvage nothing from the home itself but, perhaps out of shame, Mme. Boyer gave me access to certain items in storage. In time, I took a vanity, a piano, and living room furniture. The piano had to be sold because I had no money; other items were trucked down to Athens. They would be needed when Rachel and I were married.

Somewhat strengthened by this last development, I now took a bolder step. I went to the house by the sea, the home I loved most. At first sight its frame loomed before me, a coffinlike specter. Its spirit was gone and a palpable aura of death clung to it. I caught a glimpse of three gravestones under the balcony, and I drew near. The stones were those of my grandfather Elia Errera, and my aunt and uncle Allegra and Joseph Ezrati, Tanasaki's parents. My heart broke and my body began to quake, but I went to the door and rang the bell. When strangers answered, I fled as one on fire.

I can only guess that when the Germans uprooted the Jewish cemetery in 1941, the family sought the stones and brought them home.[2] I was told that at the time all the Jews tried to do something of the sort, and it is all I have to go on. The Greeks and Germans had been plundering the marble, and many of the gravestones were showing up on walkways and patios or in the linings of swimming pools.

I never again returned to my lifelong refuge other than in dreams. After my visit, I sold my grandfather's interest in the house for practically nothing. There were others who, like me, could no longer live in the sorrowful remains of a once-vibrant home, and they too did as I did. Ample advantage was taken of this fact, and the market was low. I did not quibble against this wrong, but the house that should have commanded the equivalent of one hundred thousand dollars instead brought in fifteen hundred. A chapter of my life had ended. The soul of the house now lives within me and I alone inhabit its rooms. I race through them with phantoms and there, upon the balcony, I still see the child I was pondering over the mystery of my grandfather casting fish back into the sea ...

The next stop was #51 Mizrahi. My parents, sister, and I had lived there from the time Sol and I were babies, and it was the only home my brother Albert had known. The new tenants were understanding and kind; they took me in, allowing me to visit each room.

2. Elia's mother, grandmother, and Guillaume could have managed this feat by themselves, but it is possible that friends brought the stones to the house as an act of kindness. (Elia knew nothing of this while he was in Athens.)

When I asked if anything that once belonged to us had remained, they looked for and found my brother's photo album.[3] After that I left, and a new wave of sorrow swept over me. Albert's album was in hand and I, beset by the past, was swarmed by memories of happier days.

3. Most of the photos represented here came from Albert's album.

I went to my father's factory. It was closed. I opened the door and found that everything was more or less as I had remembered it. The rare wines and liqueurs we had buried in the sand on the basement floor, and had aged there so patiently, were gone. The Germans had plowed everywhere and they had plundered everything. Only a few installations remained; they were practically worthless, and I sold them for very little. The barrels were dry and the wood was terribly neglected. When we tried to remove them, they fell apart.

One day when in the vicinity of the factory, I heard a man cry out: "Albert! Albert!" Someone was shouting from atop a large, horsedrawn, open wagon. I did not imagine he meant me, but he came up to ask: "Albert, don't you remember me?" It was someone who had delivered wines for my father. "I transported the bottles in this very wagon," he announced. I explained that I was not Albert, that I was Elia, and that Albert, my brother, died in a concentration camp. "You must come with me," he pleaded. "There is someone who has been waiting for you to return. He has something to give you."

I hopped onto the wagon and he took me to a wine

shop in a little village on the outskirts of Salonika, where I met an individual who had known my parents and was eager to restore to their proper owners certain items they had entrusted to him. One was a trunk, which I did not take the pains to open, and the other was a wooden box. I opened the box, but the moment I saw its contents I recoiled with a shudder. Within it were the engagement and wedding rings, bracelets and necklaces of the three families who had made up the partnership in the winery. Each item had been tagged: this is so-and-so's wedding band, and this is so-and-so's engagement ring; these belong to the Aelions, these to the Roussos, these to the Bottons. So, there it was. This is what was left of three beautiful families.

I could not take the box or any of its contents. Even though they were pressed upon me time and again with cries of "Take it! Are you crazy? They are for you!" I did not do it. I was too agitated. "Keep it! It's yours! I don't want it!" I shouted. At the time, I rejected these reminders totally—but since then I have come to regret my emotional decision. I could have been wiser. These were precious mementos; they were treasures of the heart.

I did not want to take the trunk, but no one would allow argument on this point. They simply placed it aboard the wagon, and it went back with me. In time it went to Athens, and then it came to America when Rachel and I emigrated, but never once did I open it.

The years passed, and one day I looked into it. Within, I found the wedding dresses and trousseaus of my sister, Sol, and my aunt Berta. Embroidered tablecloths, summer drapes, lamps, kitchen utensils, and many other things from my parents' home were stored in it too, and once more I was plunged into misery. I had unlocked the artifacts and dreams of a lifetime.

Some time after the incident with the box and the trunk, I went to the Sasson house. It was not only where my uncle Joseph had lived after he married Mary, but also where I had stored an enormous cache of woolen goods in the attic during the early days of the German occupation of Salonika. My funds were running out; such assets as existed had crumbled into dust, and I had to work; I had to make a living. I knew that there were survivors among the Sassons and that an uncle had taken possession of the house, so I went there to see him. I went there to wind up affairs—but human nature can be devious, and not all men allow for a straightforward account of their actions. "What woolens?" protested the uncle. He looked at me as one looks at a simpleton, and spoke as to a child. "Come here," he said. We went to the attic together. "You can see that there are no goods here—but two of Joseph's armchairs remain, and you may have them."

XIII

*Ni novia sin cejas, ni
boda sin quejas.*

Neither a bride without brows, nor
a wedding without complaint.

All during my excursions from one place to another, which were both time consuming and emotionally draining, I maintained a steady correspondence with Rachel. Each day I was able to post a letter to her, even though I may not have written anything at all on that day. I had devised a system that involved writing a series of letters in a single sitting, each of which was dated appropriately, and it worked. At the designated time, I simply mailed the communication for that day. It was a mischievous deception, and one I enjoyed thoroughly. It freed me at the same time that it connected me.

Although I had been in Salonika for a year, very little had been accomplished. The time to return to Athens had come, and I knew what awaited me there. Rachel would want to get married and I, who loved her, was not ready to do so. On my return, therefore, I did everything to delay the fateful day. "Let's get married on the fifteenth," Rachel urged, but I replied that it was too soon. "Let's get married at the beginning of the month," she said, but I replied that it was inauspicious. "Well then, how about the . . . ? " She consulted a calendar and supplied an alternative, but I replied: "Let us check our horoscopes." At last, on my final attempt at procrastination, I suggested that we marry when the moon was full. It would be romantic then.

Afterword

Not a trace remains of the house by the sea. Mizrahi Street has been renamed, and the neighborhood no longer reflects anything of the past. In Athens, scarcely anyone remembers the Atlas Hotel, or knows that during the war it served as a refuge for Jews. When inquiry was made at the Jewish Museum in Athens, none knew of it. The staff is young and the hotel is gone.

The head of the Jewish police in the Salonika ghetto and three of his siblings survived the war by going into hiding. It is believed that Rabbi Koretz was murdered in Auschwitz, but whether this is so will never be known. Hasson, one of the collaborators who assisted the Germans in obtaining whatever they wanted, survived the war and returned to Salonika. He was murdered there, but his wife, who was known to loathe and oppose him, remained unharmed. One of the Recanatis, also a collaborator, was sentenced to fifteen years' imprisonment but was released after serving eight years. His wife divorced him.

Elia and Rachel married and emigrated. They came to San Francisco, virtually penniless and knowing not a word of English. With very little help, they mastered English and were at work within two weeks of their arrival, Elia as an accountant and Rachel as a woman's fashion designer. They had two children, Sally and Victor, and eventually settled in the East Bay. Among their friends was a handful of those few who had survived the camps or lived in hiding.

Ninety-six percent of the Jews of Salonika perished.

Left: Haim and Mathilda Aelion with their three children: Albert, Sol, and Elia. It was taken at Langada, some twenty kilometers from Salonika.

Appendices

Langada and the Intensification of Pressure on the Jews

Langada was a colorful spa known for the properties of its mineral baths in relieving the discomforts of rheumatism. Its one drawback seems to have been the malaria breeding grounds of the nearby swamps. A week before departure, everyone therefore took quinine as a preventive.

Even though the spa was not far from the city, the journey took about four hours. Elia's father planned a picnic lunch and hired a *carossa,* or horse-drawn carriage, whose driver ran a regular shuttle from the city to the spa and back again. The family ate in the fields along the countryside, often accompanied by a *chalgidgi,* who sang and played the oud all the way from Salonika. Thus, therapeutic in origin, the event was treated as a festive occasion.

After the German occupation and particularly after the incident in Liberty Square on July 11, 1942, the Germans used Jewish slave labor "to clear the swamps." The men were not fed and had no access to food; they contracted malaria and typhus, had no antibiotics, and were dying by the hundreds. In a desperate effort to feed, medicate, or otherwise save them, the Jewish community mobilized itself and made every sacrifice—including that of meeting the extortion demands laid upon them (2.5 billion drachmas, or 16.7 million dollars), to no avail. Too late did they learn that everyone had been duped and consigned to death.

Ottoman Salonika Chronology

Before the Common Era

315   Salonika founded by Cassander, king of Macedonia.
168   Salonika captured by the Romans.
140   Alexandrian Jews constitute first Jewish settlement in Salonika.

After the Common Era

395   Salonika becomes a major city of the Byzantine Empire, second only to Constantinople.
904   Conquest of the city by Saracens.
1170   An organized Jewish community is in place.
1376   Central European Jews settle in the city.
1423   Salonika sold to the Venetians. Jews from northern Italy settle in the city.
1430   Conquest of the city by the Ottoman Empire.
1492   Twenty thousand Jews exiled from Spain settle in the city.
1496   Portuguese Jews settle in the city.
1536   Conversos settle in the city and reclaim their identity.
1545   Fire destroys eight thousand homes and eighteen synagogues in the Jewish quarter.
1655   Shabbetai Zvi, the false messiah, arrives in the city.
1666   Zvi and three hundred Jewish families convert to Islam.
1690   Thirty independent congregations consolidate into a single organization.
1715   Italian Jews of the merchant class settle in the city.
1890   Fire nearly destroys the Jewish quarter.
1891   First electric tram runs through Salonika.
1895   Salonika linked to Constantinople by railway line.
1912   Outbreak of the Balkan wars. Salonika captured by the Greek army.
1913   George I, king of Greece, assassinated in Salonika.

1915 Allied forces use Salonika as a base in World War I.

1917 The Great Fire decimates the city. The Jewish quarter is completely destroyed, including thirty-four synagogues and eleven schools; 53,737 Jews are left homeless.

1922 The Greeks from Asia Minor arrive en masse.

1931 Anti-Jewish riots result in the emigration of twenty thousand Jews to France and Palestine over the next few years.

1940 Seven thousand Salonikan Jews fight the Italian invasion forces along the Albanian front.

1941 Six days after the German invasion of Greece, Salonika is captured.

1942 Famine, disease, and slave labor consume the lives of thousands.

1943 Transports clear Salonika of its Jews, most of whom perish in Birkenau-Auschwitz.

1945 Some 56,000 Salonikan Jews (96%) have perished since the inception of the war. The majority of the deaths take place immediately on arrival of transports to Birkenau-Auschwitz.

1993 Approximately 1,500 Jews remain in Salonika.

—Adapted from The Foundation for the
Advancement of Sephardic Studies and Culture, Great Neck, NY.

Chronology of the Holocaust in Greece

1940

On October 28, the Italian ambassador to Athens delivers an ultimatum to surrender to Metaxa, the prime minister and dictator of Greece. He refuses to do so, and the Italians attack Greece from the Albanian border. Within five months, the Italians lose the war, and Hitler defers the plan to invade the Soviet Union in order to help the Italians secure the Balkan flank. The Greek army includes 12,896 Jews at this time, 343 of whom are officers.

1941

On April 6, the Wehrmacht and German troops charge through the Monastir Gap from Bulgaria to invade both Yugoslavia and Greece. Salonika falls on April 9, and Athens falls on April 27. Anti-Jewish measures are initiated almost immediately. Jewish Community Council members and other Jewish leaders are imprisoned; the Jewish hospital and apartments and homes of the Jews are requisitioned. By June 2, Germany, Bulgaria, and Italy proceed to carve up Greece, and the situation in the Bulgarian sector succumbs to ferocity. Tens of thousands of Greek peasants flee to Salonika and have no recourse other than to squat; the fate of the fourteen thousand Jews in the acquired territories is sealed. (By some estimates there are close to fifty thousand Jews in Salonika; by Yad Vashem's estimates there are fifty-six thousand.)

1942

Repressions continue to mount, and the debacle of Liberty Square on July 11 signals the onset of conscription for forced labor battalions. The men so affected are ill-fed and overworked—particularly in the swamp areas, where the men, unsheltered and unprotected, contract malaria and typhus. With food and medicine in short supply, the community is both alarmed and aroused. Its appeal to the Germans is met with a demand by Dieter Wisliceny for 2.5 billion old drachmas, an exorbitant amount, to be paid by December 15. The Jews of Greece rally and succeed in securing the drachmas, all the while tending to local emergencies—the most pronounced of which is the starvation of the children—little realizing the ultimate destination in store for those "freed."

1943

After the implementation of the Nuremberg Laws, Rabbi Koretz is ordered by the Germans to ensure compliance to racial restrictions in the provincial towns adjacent to Salonika; trade unions are ordered to expel their Jewish members, and all capital held by Jews is to be reported. As leverage, 104 hostages are seized on March 1. More than three hundred Jewish soldiers and one thousand other Jews join the partisans, and some groups are entirely made up of Jews; all fall under the command of either Greek or British officers. The Jewish underground warns the Jews of rumored deportation to Poland, and three thousand flee to Athens, often with the help of the Italians. By March 25, all Jews must be confined to one of three ghettos, but days before that, on March 15, the first of the transports to begin the process of emptying Salonika of its Jews leaves for Birkenau-Auschwitz. Nineteen transports in all will leave Salonika during the remainder of the year, and nearly everyone will be gassed within hours of arrival at Auschwitz. Some Jews are slated for Bergen-Belsen; they are considered to have a special status, but they do not all survive. On September 3, the Italians surrender to the Allies, but some groups surrender to the Germans and are mostly deployed to slave labor camps; others flee to join the partisans. Four thousand Italian officers and men are shot outright by the Germans. The situation in Athens worsens radically, and an intense manhunt for Jews in hiding ensues. The archbishops of Salonika and Athens call upon all Greeks to turn no Jew away, but many indeed have no need for such an appeal. To thwart the Germans, on October 7 Rabbi Barzelai destroys all Jewish communal records pertaining to the Jews of Athens and its environs and is led by Jewish partisans to a refuge in Free Greece, from where he enjoins others to continue to resist. As a consequence, SS police chief Stroop orders the registration of all Jews in the Athens area. No one shows up, and much turmoil ensues.

1944

The ferreting out of Jews does not slacken. Two transports leave from Athens and Korfu, and one leaves from Rhodes. Among these are the Jews of Iannina, whose fate is singularly poignant. The Jews in hiding continue to be protected and the partisans continue to sabotage the Germans at every turn, destroying bridges and other installations. Some are daring enough to infiltrate German ranks; attired in German uniform, partisans spy for the Greeks and the British. On October 12, Athens is liberated by British troops, and Greece soon thereafter plunges into civil war. The first intimations of the enormity of the catastrophe of the Holocaust now begin to surface. The most difficult realizations await those who have survived in hiding.

1945

By midyear a few survivors return from their ordeals in the concentration camps. Among them are several slave labor prisoners enforced into the *Sonder-kommando* at Birkenau-Auschwitz. They are young and forever changed by what they have experienced, and they tend to underplay the significant role they performed in the revolt at Birkenau. The once vibrant cultural life of the Jews of Greece has entered a new cycle, with few leaves left on a nearly barren tree. To reconstruct their lives, many emigrate.

ZESTAWIENIE LICZBOWE ŻYDÓW GRECKICH DEPORTOWANYCH, OSADZONYCH W OBOZIE I ZABITYCH W KOMORACH GAZOWYCH KL AUSCHWITZ *

Lp.	Data przybycia	Skąd	Liczba deportowanych	Numeracja mężczyzn skierowanych do obozu	Liczba mężczyzn skierowanych do obozu	Numeracja kobiet skierowanych do obozu	Liczba kobiet skierowanych do obozu	Łączna liczba mężczyzn i kobiet skierowanych do obozu	Liczba zabitych w komorach gazowych
1	2	3	4	5	6	7	8	9	10
1	20. 3. 43 r.	Saloniki	2800	109371 — 109787	417	38721 — 38912	192	609	2191
2	24. 3. 43 r.	Saloniki	2800	109896 — 110479	584	38962 — 39191	230	814	1986
3	25. 3. 43 r.	Saloniki	1901	110483 — 110941	459	39193 — 39428	236	695	1206
4	30. 3. 43 r.	Saloniki	2501	111147 — 111458	312	39623 — 39763	141	453	2048
5	3. 4. 43 r.	Saloniki	2800	112307 — 112640	334	39964 — 40221	258	592	2208
6	9. 4. 43 r.	Saloniki	2500	112974 — 113291	318	40280 — 40440	161	479	2021
7	10. 4. 43 r.	Saloniki	2750	114094 — 114630	537	40537 — 40782	246	783	1967
8	13. 4. 43 r.	Saloniki	2800	114875 — 115374	500	40841 — 41204	364	864	1936
9	17. 4. 43 r.	Saloniki	3000	115848 — 116314	467	41354 — 41615	262	729	2271
10	18. 4. 43 r.	Saloniki	2501	116317 — 116676	360	41616 — 41860	245	605	1896
11	22. 4. 43 r.	Saloniki	2800	117199 — 117453	255	42038 — 42450	413	668	3132
12	26. 4. 43 r.	Saloniki	2700	118425 — 118869	445	42882 — 43074	193	638	2062
13	28. 4. 43 r.	Saloniki	3070	118888 — 119067	180	43123 — 43483	361	541	2529
14	4. 5. 43 r.	Saloniki	2930	119781 — 120090	220	43779 — 44096	318	538	2392
15	7. 5. 43 r.	Saloniki	1000	— —		44259 — 44326	68	68	932
16	8. 5. 43 r.	Saloniki	2500	120650 — 121217	568	44380 — 44626	247	815	1685
17	16. 5. 43 r.	Saloniki	4500	121910 — 122375	466	44934 — 45144	211	677	3823
18	8. 6. 43 r.	Saloniki	880	124325 — 124544	220	45995 — 46082	88	308	572
19	18. 8. 43 r.	Saloniki	1000	136919 — 137189	271	— —		271	1529
20	11. 4. 44 r.	Ateny	1500	182640 — 182789	330	numery nie znane	113	433	1067
21	30. 6. 44 r.	Ateny i Korfu	2000	A15229—A15674	446	A8282—A8412	131	577	1423
22	16. 8. 44 r.	wyspa Rodos	2500	B7199 — B7304	346	A24215—A24468	254	600	1900
	Łącznie		54533		8825		4732	12757	41776

* Opracowanie autorki na podstawie biletów kolejowych, wykazów numerowych transportów więźniarskich, listy kwarantanny obozu męskiego KL Auschwitz II (Birkenau) w konfrontacji z arkuszami personalnymi więźniów, wykazem · więźniarek wybranych w dniu 21. 8. 1943 r. na śmierć w komorach

Reproduced from the original in Auschwitz.

Photocopy with the Magnes Museum in Berkeley, California.

Transports from Greece

Numerical Summary of Greek Jews Deported, Placed in Camp,

and Killed in Auschwitz*

Sequential number	Date of arrival	From	Number deported	Numbers assigned to men directed to camp
1	20.3.43 r.	Saloniki	2800	109371–109787
2	24.3.43 r.	Saloniki	2800	109896–110479
3	25.3.43 r.	Saloniki	1901	110483–110941
4	30.3.43 r.	Saloniki	2501	111147–111458
5	3.4.43 r.	Saloniki	2800	112307–112640
6	9.4.43 r.	Saloniki	2500	112974–113291
7	10.4.43 r.	Saloniki	2750	114094–114630
8	13.4.43 r.	Saloniki	2800	114875–115374
9	17.4.43 r.	Saloniki	3000	115848–116314
10	18.4.43 r.	Saloniki	2501	116317–116676
11	22.4.43 r.	Saloniki	2800	117199–117453
12	26.4.43 r.	Saloniki	2700	118425–118869
13	28.4.43 r.	Saloniki	3070	118888–119067
14	4.5.43 r.	Saloniki	2930	119781–120090
15	7.5.43 r	Saloniki	1000	— —
16	8.5.43 r	Saloniki	2500	120650–121217
17	16.5.43 r.	Saloniki	4500	121910–122375
18	8.6.43 r.	Saloniki	880	124325–124544
19	18.8.43 r.	Saloniki	1800	136919–137189
20	11.4.44 r.	Ateny	1500	182440–182789
21	30.6.44 r.	Ateny i Korfu	2000	A15229–A15674
22	16.8.44 r.	wyspa Rodos	2500	B7159–B7504
		Lacznie	54533	

* Worksheet arrived at by the authors [SS and Gestapo] on the basis of railroad tickets, numerical indications of prison transports, lists of the quarantined in the men's camp KL Auschwitz 2 (Birkenau) upon confrontation of personal sheets of prisoners, indications of women prisoners chosen on August 21, 1943, for death in the gas chamber.

Number of those men	Nos. of women assigned to camp	Number of those women	Total men and women	No. killed in gas chambers
417	38721–38912	192	609	2191
584	38962–39191	230	814	1986
459	39193–39428	236	695	1206
312	39623–39763	141	453	2048
334	39964–40221	258	592	2208
318	40280–40440	161	479	2021
537	40537–40782	246	783	1967
500	40841–41204	364	864	1936
467	41354–41615	262	729	2271
360	41616–41860	245	605	1896
255	42038–42450	413	668	3132
445	42882–43074	193	638	2062
180	43123–43483	361	541	2529
220	43779–44096	318	538	2392
—	44259–44326	68	68	932
568	44380–44626	247	815	1685
466	44934–45144	211	677	3823
220	45995–46082	88	308	572
271	— —	—	271	1529
320	numbers unknown	113	433	1067
446	A8282–A8412	131	577	1423
346	A24215–A24468	254	600	1900
8025		4732	12757	41776

Translated from Polish

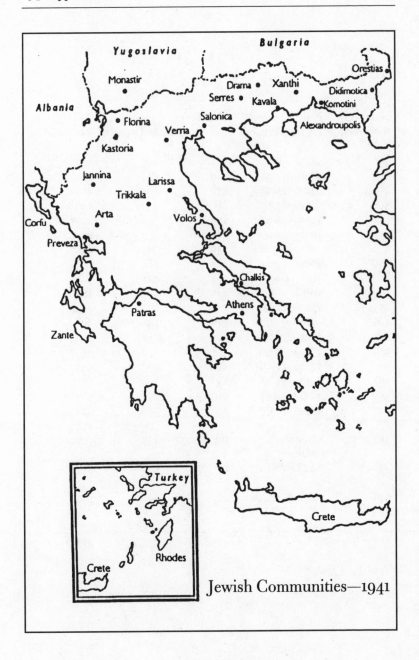

Jewish Communities—1941

Destruction of Jewish Communties

Jewish Communities	Population 1941	Population 1945	Percentage of Loss
THRACE			
1. Didimotica	900	33	99%
2. Orestias	197	3	98%
3. Alexandroupolis	140	4	97%
4. Komotini	819	28	96%
5. Xanthi	550	6	99%
MACEDONIA			
6. Kavala	2,100	42	98%
7. Drama	1,200	39	97%
8. Serres	600	3	99%
9. Salonica	56,000	1,950	96%
10. Verria	460	131	72%
11. Kastoria	900	35	96%
12. Florina	400	64	84%
THESSALY			
13. Trikkala	520	360	31%
14. Larissa	1,120	726	35%
15. Volos	872	645	26%
OLD GREECE			
16. Chalkis	325	170	48%
17. Athens*	3,000	4,930	+64%
PELOPONNESE			
18. Patras-Agrinion	265	152	43%
EPIRUS			
19. Jannina	1,850	163	91%
20. Preveza	250	15	94%
21. Arta	384	60	84%
THE ISLANDS			
22. Corfu	2,000	185	91%
23. Zante	275	275	—
24. Crete	350	7	98%
25. Rhodes	1,701	40	89%
TOTAL	77,178	10,066	89%

*NOTE: The loss within the Athens Jewish Community was 1,000 individuals. The postwar increase is attributed to the number of Jewish refugees who remained in the city.

Source: Black Book of Localities whose Jewish population was Exterminated by the Nazis. Yad Vashem. Jerusalem, 1965.

OSS[1] Document RG226

1. Office of Strategic Services.
The precursor to the Central Intelligence Agency (CIA).

Commentary

The information in OSS Document RG226 was obtained in a debriefing interview with two Greek students who fled Salonika with nineteen others on August 5, 1943. The students were interviewed by the OSS in Istanbul on August 7, 1943. Copies of the document were sent to the OSS field headquarters in Izmir and Cairo as well as to the U.S. Navy and the OSS in Washington, where it was received on September 7, 1943. It does not appear to have been disseminated within the U.S. government or to the Greek government. The students seem to have been well informed, but whether they were merely keen observers, as distinct from spies for the Allies, and whether they were fleeing the raids referred to in item 4 are matters of pure speculation.

Items 1, 2, 3, and 5 give a clear indication of Salonika's importance to the Germans as a military depot, while item four indicates the lengths to which the Germans went to secure slave labor among the general male population once the Jews of Salonika had been routed and sent to their deaths. The disposition of the goods confiscated from Jewish businesses and households is specified in item 6, but item 6 is of great significance on other counts as well, for it makes clear that German officers knew and freely acknowledged that the Jews were being gassed. The terms they used were typically cynical: *Jews were forced in large groups to enter an empty cleaning establishment, and from there were sent to heaven.* What is particularly damning in item 6, however, is the fact that the "natives of Salonika" did not believe any of the Jews would return. This, then, was an open secret, a secret shared with the students and known to the general population.

The report reflects some confusion as to where the Greek Jews were put to death, and the reference to Serbia is in this instance incorrect. Such deaths did occur in gas vans in Serbia and elsewhere in 1942, but this method was too inefficient for the scale envisioned by the Germans.

It should be noted that RG226 lists the names of several Greeks who were agents of the Gestapo in Salonika. Among them is one Periklis Nikolaidis. Elia

Aelion has informed me that Nikolaidis is a common Greek name, and that the Mrs. Nikolaidis who looked after him and Rachel was not known to have relatives in Salonika.

The overall importance of the document attests to the fact that clear information as to the determined extermination of the Jews was known to Allied policy makers in 1943. Had action been taken—although too late for the Jews of Greece—millions of lives could have been saved and countless suffering avoided by the war's end in 1945.

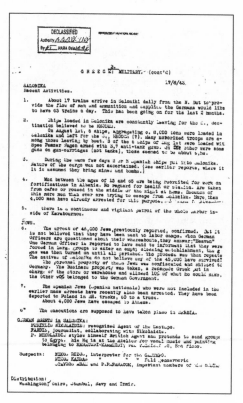

Declassified January 9, 1998.
Reproduced from the original at the National Archives, Washington, D.C.

3. GREECE: MILITARY. (cont.)

SALONIKA   17/8/43

Recent Activities.

1. About 17 trains arrive in Saloniki daily from the N. But to provide the flow of men and ammunition and supplies the Germans would like to have 65 trains a day. This has been going on for the last 2 months.

2. Ships loaded in Salonika are constantly leaving for the S., destination believed to be RHODES.

On August 1st, 6 ships, aggregating c. 8,000 tons, were loaded in Salonika and left for the S., RHODES (?). Many motorized troops are among those leaving by boat. 3 of the 6 ships of Aug. 1st were loaded with Spee Panzer Wagen armed with 3,7 anti-tank guns. On another were some guns on gun-carriages (not tanks), these seemed to be about 6,5s.

3. During the same few days 2 or 3 Spanish ships put into Salonika. Nature of the cargo was not ascertained. (see earlier reports, where it is assumed they bring mines and bombs.)

4. Men between the ages of 15 and 65 are being recruited for work on fortifications in Albania. No regard for health or station. Are taken from cafés or roused in the middle of the night at home. Because of this more men than ever are trying to escape from Salonika. More than 4,000 men have already arrested for this purpose and sent to Albania.

5. There is a continuous and vigilant patrol of the whole harbor inside Karabournou.

JEWS

6. The arrest of 45,000 Jews, previously reported, confirmed. But it is not believed that they have been sent to labor camps. When German Officers are questioned about their whereabouts, they answer; "Heaven." One German Officer is reported to have said to informant that they were forced in large groups to enter an empty cleaning establishment, the gas was then turned on until all per-

ished. The process was then repeate[d]. The natives of Salonika do not believe any of the 45,000 have survived.

The personal property (i.e. household) of these Jews was confiscated and shipped to Germany. The Business property was taken, the renegade Greek put in charge of the store or warehouse and allowed 10% of what he could make, the other 90% belonged to the German Government.

7. The Spanish Jews (Spanish nationals) who were not included in the earlier mass arrests have recently also been arrested. They have been deported to Poland in RR. trucks, 80 to a truck.

About 4,000 Jews have escaped to Athens.

8. The executions are supposed to have taken place in SERBIA.

GERMAN AGENTS IN SALONIKA:

PERIKLIS NIKOLAIDIS: recognized Agent of the Gestapo.

FARDIS, journalist, collaborating with Nikolaidis.

P. NIKOLAIDIS styles himself British Agent and pretends to send groups to Egypt. His HQ is at the Atelier for vocal music and painting belonging to HARATARI-KARAZISI, rue TSIMISKI 32, 3rd floor.

Suspects:

NIKOS RIZOS, interpreter for the GESTAPO.

NIKOS KARRAS, interpreter for the Feld gendarmerie.

STAVROS ADAM and P. PAPANAOUM, important members of the GESTAPO.

Distribution:
Washington, Cairo, Stambul, Navy and Izmir.

Glossary

Auschwitz. The entire Auschwitz complex was made up of three camps, which were often referred to as Auschwitz I, Auschwitz II, and Auschwitz III. The main camp, Auschwitz I, was about two miles from Birkenau, or Auschwitz II. Monowitz-Buna, or Auschwitz III, was approximately five miles farther from Birkenau. Each camp had satellites or sub-camps, some as many as three hundred; these utilized the Jews and others as slave laborers and built up the German war industries.

Gestapo headquarters, the "hospital" in which Joseph Mengele experimented on his victims, the prison, and one essentially defunct crematorium were in the main camp. The main killing center was in Birkenau, which had four gas chambers and crematoria and five massive pits in which bodies were burned. A huge industrial complex generating fuel and experimenting on the manufacture of synthetic rubber was housed in Monowitz-Buna, which exploited some sixty thousand slave laborers, one of whom was Primo Levi.

Erev Yom Kippur. Eve of the Day of Atonement.

Gestapo (Geheime Staatspolizei). Secret state police employing methods considered underhanded; a symbol of the Nazi terror.

Kehillah. Synagogue.

Ladino. Judeo-Spanish, the language of the Sephardim. Fifteenth-century Spanish which, over the centuries, acquired words and idioms from the Hebrew, Turkish, Arabic, French, and Italian languages.

Megillah. Scroll of Esther. A written account read during Purim. The saga of the Jewess Esther, a woman of beauty and valor, who became the bride of Ahasuerus, King of Persia. As queen, she saved the Jews from the persecution devised for them by Haman, the king's counselor, by revealing her true identity at a crucial moment in the fate of her people. Esther, associated with Ishtar, the goddess of fertility, is referred to as Saint Esther by Crypto Jews, a branch of the Sephardim cut off from the mainstream of Jewish life as a result of the Inquisitions of 1492 and 1497 and subsequent events.

Pesach or Passover. A period set aside for the recounting of the Exodus out of Egypt and an exploration of its significance past and present.

Purim. A period of festivity celebrating the reversal of Haman's decree and the punishment meted out to him. A time for costumes, parties, special pastries, treats for children, and beauty pageants. See photos pp. 31, 50.

Rosh Hashanah. The beginning of the year, marking the onset of a ten-day period set aside for individual and communal reflection. A time of rectification. A new start for the new year.

Seder. The format and symbols used to commemorate the Exodus, and a time to explore issues of freedom, slavery, or oppression near and far. The gathering of friends and family for this purpose. A dinnertime event lasting long into the night.

Selection. A means of achieving a dual objective by exploiting those strong or well enough to work and exterminating them at will or when their usefulness came to an end. The culling out of the vulnerable for purposes of medical or other experiments. A method of entrapment in an anarchic or systematic raid. A euphemism for the process of choosing victims for the gas chambers whenever a new transport arrived in a Nazi concentration camp so equipped, and an ongoing process in the camps in the fulfillment of a genocidal aim.

Sephardi; Sephardim (pl.). A Jew who can trace his roots to pre-Inquisition Spain.

Shabbat. Sabbath. Saturday. A day of rest and reflection or study. Separation from the workaday world and its cares.

Sonderkommando. Euphemism literally meaning "special detail." A term whose significance and application evolved exponentially as the refinements of genocidal intent were articulated and increasingly set into motion. Ultimately, under the watchful eye of the SS, the use of teams of slave labor prisoners who were made to participate in the disposal of their own people after they had been gassed or otherwise murdered, most notoriously at Birkenau-Auschwitz.

Sport or sports. Euphemism for the exercise of power over another through the infliction of a grueling form of physical exertion, often leading to dire consequences or actual death. An ironic usage employed by the Germans in the Second World War to mask contempt and engender humiliation.

SS (Schutzstaffel). Usually written with two runic lightning symbols. Elite guard of the Nazis initially, but much expanded under Himmler to include such areas as the resettlement of populations, the conduct of the war, and the destruction of the Jews. Akin to the police. A civil service party amalgamation, whose chiefs were accountable to Himmler. Killers implementing the final solution. Operators and/or deployers of mobile killing units. Instigators of massacres, etc. Hunters of men, using vicious dogs to track, maim, subdue, or kill their prey.

Succot. A harvest festival. Precursor to Thanksgiving.

Yad Vashem. The phrase Yad Vashem first appears in Isaiah 56:5, where it signifies a monument and a memorial. It refers to the name adopted by the Holocaust memorial and archival center in Jerusalem, Israel.

Yom Kippur. The Day of Atonement; the last of the ten days from Rosh Hashanah in which to make amends to one another.

Suggested Reading

Berenbaum, Michael, ed. *Witness to the Holocaust* (New York: Harper Collins Publishers, 1997).

Cohen, Leon. *From Greece to Birkenau: The Crematoria Workers' Uprising* (Jerusalem: Graphit Press Ltd., 1996).

Fromer, Rebecca. *The Holocaust Odyssey of Daniel Bennahmias, Sonderkommando* (Tuscaloosa and London: University of Alabama Press, 1993).

Gaon, Salomon and Serels, Mitchell M., eds. *Sephardim and the Holocaust* (New York: Jacob E. Safra Institute of Sephardic Studies, Yeshiva University, 1987).

Gilbert, Martin. *The Holocaust: A History of the Jews of Europe During the Second World War* (New York: Holt, Rinehart, and Winston, 1985).

Gutman, Yisrael and Berenbaum, Michael, eds. *Anatomy of the Auschwitz Death Camp* (Bloomington and Indianapolis: Indiana University Press, 1994).

Hilberg, Raul. *The Destruction of the European Jews* (New York and London: Holmes and Meier, 1985).

Kantor, Alfred. *The Book of Alfred Kantor* (New York: McGraw-Hill, 1971).

Levi, Primo. *Survival in Auschwitz* (London: Collier Macmillan, 1959).

Matza, Diane, ed. *Sephardic-American Voices* (Hanover and London: Univer-sity Press of New England, 1997).

Mazower, Mark. *Inside Hitler's Greece: The Experience of Occupation 1941–44* (New Haven and London: Yale University Press, 1993).

Molho, René. *They Say Diamonds Don't Burn* (Berkeley: Magnes Museum, 1994).

Müller, Filip. *Eyewitness Auschwitz* (New York: Stein and Day, 1979).

Nahon, Marco. Birkenau, *The Camp of Death* (Tuscaloosa and London: University of Alabama Press, 1989).

Plaut, Joshua Eli. *Greek Jewry in the Twentieth Century, 1913–1983, Patterns of Jewish Survival in the Greek Provinces Before and After the Holocaust* (Cranbury: Associated University Press, 1996).

Roth, John K. and Berenbaum, Michael, eds. *Holocaust: Religious & Philosophical Implications* (St. Paul: Paragon House, 1989).

Rebecca Camhi Fromer's parents, Jack Camhi and Sarah Castro, met in Salonika and were married there shortly before the First World War. Of her devotion to Holocaust work, Fromer has said (in Diane Matza, ed., *Sephardic-American Voices: Two Hundred Years of a Literary Legacy,* Hanover: Brandeis University Press, 1997), "Memorable to me was the valiant effort of one of my father's brothers-in-law, who came to the United States under the pretext of visiting the New York World's Fair in 1939. He could enter by no other means, and he was in earnest to pursue the matter of exit visas for the family-now grown quite large. They were aware of Hitler's threats, and they took them seriously, but all efforts at emigration failed. The State Department was implacable, the man returned, and everyone perished. Whoever remained in Greece on my mother's side also perished. Now these factors, along with the larger implications of the Holocaust, affected me profoundly; they shaped my consciousness, and they influenced what I do." Fromer is the author of *The Holocaust Odyssey of Daniel Bennahmias, Sonderkommando,* and co-founder of the Judah L. Magnes Memorial Museum in Berkeley, California. A teacher, poet, and playwright, she is married with one daughter. She lives in Berkeley. (Photograph © Peg Skorpinski).